Kafka

Reading Aloud, drawing of Kafka by Friedrich Feigl

John Hibberd

Kafka

in context

Studio Vista

KEY TO ABBREVIATIONS

BR.   *Briefe 1902–1924* (1966)
BRF.   *Briefe an Felice* (1967)
BRM.   *Briefe an Milena* (1952)
BK.   *Beschreibung eines Kampfes* (1946)
E.   *Erzählungen und Kleine Prosa* (1946)
H.   *Hochzeitsvorbereitungen auf dem Lande* (1953)
T.   *Tagebücher 1910–1923* (1951)
BROD.   Max Brod, *Franz Kafka, Eine Biographie* (1954)
J.   Gustav Janouch, *Gespräche mit Kafka* (1961)

AUTHOR'S NOTE

Quotations are taken from the authorized translations of Kafka by permission of Schocken Books Inc. and Secker and Warburg Ltd, and from *Conversations with Kafka* by permission of Andre Deutsch Ltd. Extracts from Kafka's *Briefe 1902–1924*, translated by myself, are printed by permission of Schocken Books Inc., copyright © Schocken Books Inc., 1974. I wish to thank those who have helped and encouraged me in writing this book, particularly my wife, Estelle and Michael Morgan, Hans Reiss.

ILLUSTRATION ACKNOWLEDGEMENTS

Illustrations on pages 2, 8, 9, 13, 16, 20, 30, 35, 63, 66, 88, 91, 92, 101, 105, 109, 111, 131, 132 Akademie der Künste, Berlin, courtesy Dr Klaus Wagenbach; pages 27, 29, 37 Albertina, Vienna; page 125 BBC copyright photograph; pages 53, 54, 55, 56 British Film Institute, London; page 121 Deutsches Institut fur Filmkunde, Frankfurt; pages 26, 85, 114 Marlborough Fine Art, London; page 47 Nasjonalgalleriet, Oslo; page 17 Paul Popper Ltd, London; page 81 Royal Geographical Society, London; pages 133, 139 Staatsgalerie, Stuttgart; page 67 Stadt Kunstsammlung, Gelsenkirchen; page 115 Stedelijk Museum, Amsterdam; pages 48, 123 *Drawings to Kafka* by Yosl Bergnes pub. Tarshish Books, Jerusalem 1959; page 25 Tate Gallery, London, © SPADEM; page 21 Wallraf-Richartz-Museum, Cologne, © SPADEM

Studio Vista
Cassell & Collier Macmillan Publishers Limited
35 Red Lion Square, London WC1R 4SG
Copyright © John Hibberd 1975
Picture research by Annette Brown
Designed by Gillian Greenwood
All rights reserved. No part of this publication
may be reproduced, stored in a retrieval system,
or transmitted, in any form or by any means, electronic,
mechanical, photocopying, recording or otherwise, without
the prior permission of Studio Vista
First published in Great Britain 1975
ISBN 0 289 70498 7 (paperback)
ISBN 0 289 70499 5 (hardback)
Set in Monotype Perpetua
Printed in Great Britain by
Fletcher & Son Ltd, Norwich

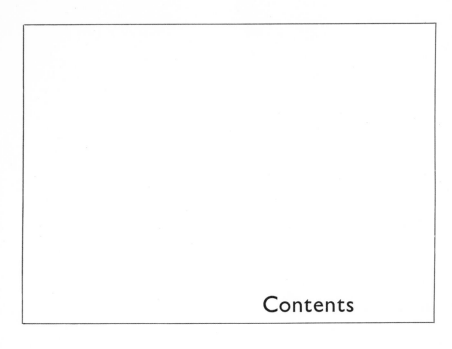

Contents

Introduction

Franz Kafka's life was a private tragedy mingled with farce, almost as strange and terrible as that of any of his fictional heroes. His biography is a story of mental conflict and torment which he himself recorded in his diaries and letters with the genius of a great writer and the scrupulous accuracy of a hypochondriac and introvert. He paints a compelling self-portrait of a man unfit for life who failed miserably in all his endeavours. The knowledge that his problems arose from his mentality as much as from external circumstances did not help him solve them, for his mind was to him more real than anything else in the world. His searching vision was turned inwards. From the city of Prague he observed, yet apparently all but ignored, the historic events of his time, the Great War, the collapse of the Austro-Hungarian Empire, the birth of Czechoslovakia. He believed that his pronounced individuality, his vocation as a writer and his Jewishness made him an outsider. From a position of isolation he created stories of estrangement for which he has become famous.

He was a very reticent person and few knew him well. Many of his relatives and friends died before public interest in his work was aroused, several as victims of the Nazi terror. His best friend, Max Brod, has written a sympathetic account of Kafka as man and writer which in part corrects Kafka's own self-analysis. While Kafka emphasized his own peculiarity, others have seen his fate as typical of the homeless Jew and the individual deprived of spiritual certainty. Kafka himself, indeed, knew that his life was intimately involved with the history of modern Europe.

Analogies with others who lived in tortured solitude, exposed to philosophical or emotional crisis, sensitive to the absurdity of life, with Kierkegaard, Dostoyevsky, Nietzsche, Sartre and Camus, help us to understand his predicament. And Kafka is inseparable from Prague and his time. The illustrations to this volume indicate some of the moods and themes that he shared with other artists, particularly his contemporaries, the Expressionists. His work has, indeed, the direct visual impact of Expressionist and Surrealist art, while its intellectual searching has affinities with Existentialism.

Kafka published little during his lifetime. Only a few perceptive minds appreciated the quality of his writing. His three novels and most of his stories existed only as fragments in manuscript when he died in 1924. Max Brod, convinced of his friend's genius, ignored Kafka's instructions to burn this material and prepared it for publication. Some years after the author's death his narratives were read with enthusiasm by fellow writers, they fascinated intellectuals and later captivated a more general public all over the world. He has been universally acknowledged as a writer of great insight and sensitivity who gave significant expression to problems which have been felt to be particularly acute in the modern world. Yet there was and still is considerable disagreement about the meaning of his works. He has been acclaimed as a religious writer: for some he writes of religious despair, the absurdity of life and the impossibility of belief; for some he expresses fundamental truths and a moving faith. Others have seen his works as psychological studies of an isolated individual, or the Jew in exile, or modern man in general. Some find social and political meanings in his stories, and others still believe that in his writings he was concerned with the limitations of language and thought, or with the task of writing itself. More recently there has been some agreement that his work allows and even requires many different interpretations and that this all-pervasive ambiguity itself is his achievement and his comment on the world.

Kafka himself stressed the links between his personality and his writing. The biographical approach to his fiction tells us much, but does not lead to a complete or final understanding of it. His stories are not simply disguised autobiography or confession but imaginative creations: however much they are based on one man's experience they have wider implications. It is these wider meanings that make him so significant as one of the greatest explorers of spiritual problems in our century.

Hermann Kafka's trademark: a jackdaw (czeck *kavka*)

Formative years

After reading the many pessimistic and self-deprecatory passages in Franz Kafka's letters and diaries one is inclined to think that, in his view, his birth on 3 July 1883 in the city of Prague was the first mistake of his life and an error for which he, with his mastery of moral subtlety, might well have blamed himself. He could, indeed, have chosen a better time and place to be born a Jew. In another age and another society he might not have felt so acutely the insecurity which was to torment him. But the adult Kafka did not need to look beyond his own family for the conditions which, he felt, had determined his personality. He was, he believed, born with many of the characteristics of his mother's family and only a few of his father's; this meant that he was unable to live up to his father's expectations and incurred his disapproval and even hatred. Kafka saw almost all his actions as an attempt to prove his own worth to his father or to free himself from him. Only a couple of years before his death in 1924 he was to write in his diary that as a child he had been defeated by his father, and ever since had been driven by ambition to continue the battle and to suffer perpetual defeats (T. 2.12.'21).

His father, Hermann Kafka (1852–1931), a butcher's son, was born in a hamlet in southern Bohemia and spent his childhood in a one-room

8

cottage that housed a family of eight. As a boy he often went barefoot through the winter snow as he delivered meat to Jewish families in the surrounding countryside. At the age of fourteen he left home to scrape a living as a pedlar. After a period of military service he moved to Prague, in the wake of many Jews who since their legal emancipation in 1848 hoped to make their fortune in the city. In 1882 he married Julie Löwy who came from a well-to-do and educated family of

Kafka's mother

German Jews. Hard work and ambition enabled him to rise from small beginnings as a dealer in haberdashery and fancy goods, and the frequent moves from one flat to another experienced by the young Franz marked a steady improvement in his father's financial position and a noticeable rise in social status. His Jewishness and his humble origin were obstacles to Hermann Kafka's desire to ascend the social scale. Even greater handicaps were his provincial background and his mother-tongue, Czech. For under Austrian rule social advancement in Prague was possible only via the German-speaking minority (some 34,000 of a total 450,000 inhabitants in 1900). The Germans of Bohemia took it for granted that they were part of the ruling race in the Habsburg Empire. The Czechs were scarcely regarded as equals by the aristocrats, businessmen and civil servants whose cultural roots were in Vienna and western Europe. In his early years in Prague Hermann Kafka became accepted by the Czech population: once his shop was saved from the attentions of anti-Semites when passers-by declared that he was Czech. Yet he forsook this relative security and aspired to become part of the German-speaking élite. He changed his place of worship from a Czech-speaking to a German synagogue, sent his children to German schools and for a time, until the political situation changed, used as his business emblem a jackdaw (Czech *kavka* – jackdaw) perched on a sprig of German oak.

A self-made man of the nineteenth century, Hermann Kafka had an authoritarian concept of his role as head of the family and decidedly bourgeois views on the virtue of hard work and on the importance of social standing. He worked long hours and his children saw him mostly at meal times or as the ultimate disciplinary authority. He had little understanding of his son's sensitivity and intended to bring him up harshly to equip him for a harsh world. Not that he used corporal punishment, for the mere threat of this was enough to terrify the boy. Franz was hurt quite enough by his father's constant references to the hardships of his own youth which implied that his child was not sufficiently grateful for a comfortable home. More serious perhaps for Kafka's psychological development was his father's failure to explain or justify his parental edicts, which were often incomprehensible to the son. The son's confusion only increased when the father demanded adherence to standards that he himself ignored, for instance in table manners. Hermann Kafka had, as his son was later to note, many of the characteristics of a tyrant. The inconsistency, incomprehensibility and apparent unworthiness of the various authorities and their representatives in Kafka's novels and stories may well reflect his experience of his father, the first authority in his life.

Such was Hermann Kafka as seen by his son. In reality he was probably rather more benign. He did find time to take Franz swimming, an activity that Kafka was later to enjoy; but in his father's presence he was so overwhelmed by his own poor physique, as compared with the tall imposing figure of his parent, that he was quite miserable. It was his misery as a child that he later recalled vividly, and he may have distorted facts in the act of recollection. We know little more than is revealed by Kafka himself, and our chief source, the *Letter to My Father* which he wrote in 1919 but which never reached Hermann Kafka, abounds, as the writer was to confess, in the artifices of a counsel for the defence (BRM. 80). Kafka there extends apparent sympathy only to accuse, saying that his father could only treat a child according to his own nature, with vigour, noise and violent temper (H. 166). Hermann Kafka did not have such a devastating effect on his daughters, although the youngest, Ottla, shared her brother's dislike of his tyrannical traits. But as the only son Franz was expected, according to a pattern particularly pronounced in Jewish families, to fulfil his father's hopes and aspirations, and he saw this expectation as a duty imposed upon him. But it was not just a duty: Kafka longed for his father's approval and love.

Kafka soon realized that he lacked his father's strength of will – or rather his clarity of purpose (for Franz was uncommonly obdurate in many matters) – and was convinced that his father rejected his otherness, as did the family as a whole: 'My peculiarity was not accorded any recognition; but since I felt it, I could not fail – being very sensitive on this score and always suspicious – to recognize adverse criticism in this attitude to me. But if even this openly displayed peculiarity met with condemnation, how much worse then must those peculiarities be which I kept concealed for the reason that I myself recognized something a little wrong in them' (H. 229). From his own experience Kafka created an archetypal parent whose sole desire was to have a child who would follow him in his ambitions and succeed where he had failed. When his sister Elli married he urged her to send her children to boarding school and thus remove them from the destructive influence of parents. The basis of all parental attitudes, he wrote, was a selfishness that knew no limits. Even the parent who loved his child with all his heart was more selfish than the most unfeeling teacher, nor could it be otherwise. In bringing up his child, the parent notices in him characteristics that he hates in himself; he hopes to remove them from the child, and so sets to work to change him. Invariably, too, he thinks that the child lacks something he regards as an excellence in himself and essential in the family, and attempts to hammer this quality into him. Whatever success he might have in changing the child is illusory, for in educating him he destroys him, smashes his individuality (BR. 345). Despite these views, Kafka was to long for a child of his own.

Kafka also blamed his father for instilling into him distrust of others and of himself: 'The mistrust that you tried to instil into me towards most people (name me a single person who was of importance to me in my childhood whom you didn't at least once tear to shreds with your criticism) . . . This mistrust (which was nowhere confirmed in the eyes of the little boy, since everywhere I saw only people excellent beyond any hope of emulation) turned in me to mistrust of myself and perpetual anxiety of everything else' (H. 196). Since no one, least of all himself, measured up to his father's standards, and he did not dare to question the rightness of his father's views which he could not understand, he developed a sense of insecurity and inferiority, and a tendency to self-criticism. His father's sarcasms seemed to show that he attached no importance to his son's feelings and opinions. Kafka dared not count on a predictable future: he wrote that he had been so uncertain of everything that he felt he possessed only what was already in his hands or his mouth or was at least on its way there (H. 191).

Kafka's mother was more considerate and sympathetic but he felt that she never really understood him. He recalled how comforting she could be and how she must have suffered, exposed to the will of her husband and the demands of her children. She was expected to assist in the family business and to join her husband at cards in the evening, so she too had little time to devote to her children. In matters of discipline she was often more liberal than her husband, but in turning a blind eye to certain misdeeds she only encouraged the boy's sense of guilt when he compared his behaviour with his father's standards.

Julie Kafka's family included men known for their piety, rabbis, intellectuals and doctors, and several cranks. Kafka felt greater sympathy for these relatives than for those on his father's side and liked to think that he had inherited their characteristics, which he saw as intellectualism and individualism and a tendency to poor health. With morbid satisfaction he noted that his maternal grandmother had died of typhoid when relatively young and that her mother had committed

Kafka's uncle, Siegfried Löwy

suicide. Physical and emotional inability to stand up to the rigours of life had, he believed, been passed down to him. His mother's brothers were attractive to him because they had broken away from the narrow bounds of conformism. His favourite uncle, Siegfried, a doctor in a country district of Moravia, was a fanatical believer in fresh air. Kafka himself shared this fad and kept his window open even in the coldest weather. He also wore light clothes throughout the year, presumably to allow the air to get to his body. Another uncle, Alfred, became director-general of the Spanish railways in Madrid. Kafka's uncle Rudolf was converted to Catholicism. His uncle Josef set up a trading post in the Congo and later settled in Paris; Kafka regarded him as another unconventional and adventurous spirit. With such relations in mind he added to the characteristics of his mother's family restlessness, sensitivity, and, for reasons that are not so clear (though it is often considered a strong Jewish trait), a pronounced sense of justice.

Franz was the eldest child. Two brothers died in infancy, and his three sisters, Elli, Valli and Ottla, were so much younger – six, seven and nine years respectively – that they provided no companionship in his childhood. The loneliness of his early years increased his natural tendency to introspection and shyness. The household servants, a kindly maid who stood in fear of his father, a cook who was a strict disciplinarian, and later a French governess (a sign of social status), were little more to the child than representatives of parental authority. His emotional insecurity took the form of extreme self-consciousness. Although probably well dressed he was convinced that his clothes were badly made and drew attention to him and was quite sure that he cut a miserable figure in public (T. 3.12.'11).

In 1889 he was sent to the German elementary school. The walk to school was a nightmare that became only half-comic in recollection:

> Our cook, a small dry thin person . . ., firm, energetic and superior, led me every morning to school. . . . And now every morning for about a year the same thing was repeated. At the moment of leaving the house the cook said she would tell the teacher how naughty I'd been at home. As a matter of fact I probably wasn't very naughty, but rather stubborn, useless, sad, bad-tempered, and out of all this probably something quite nice could have been fabricated for the teacher. I knew this, so didn't take the cook's threat too lightly. All the same since the road to school was enormously long I believed at first that anything might happen on the way. . . . I was also very much in doubt . . . as to whether the cook, though a person commanding respect if only in domestic quarters, would dare to talk to the world-respect-commanding person of the teacher. . . . Somewhere near the entrance to the Fleischmarktgasse . . . fear of the threat got the upper hand. School in itself was already enough of a nightmare, and now the cook was trying to make it even worse. I began to plead, she shook her head, the more I pleaded the more precious appeared to me that for which I was pleading, the greater the danger;

I stood still and begged forgiveness, she dragged me along, I threatened with retaliation from my parents, she laughed. . . . I held on to the shop doors, to the corner stones, I refused to go any further until she had forgiven me, but she kept dragging me along with the assurance that she would tell the teacher this, too, it grew late. . . . I always had the greatest terror of being late. . . . She didn't tell, ever, but she always had the opportunity and even an apparently increasing opportunity . . . (BrM. 64 f.)

On the way he passed a Czech school at whose entrance he read the words of the educationist Comenius: 'A Czech child belongs in a Czech school.' Now, if not before, he became aware of the tension between the Czech and German-speaking populations of Prague. His father, like most Germans in the city, pretended to ignore this situation, but it was common for schoolchildren to engage in street fights, Czechs against Germans. Kafka's later friend, the writer Oskar Baum, lost his sight in such a schoolboy battle in Prague, and Kafka commented sadly that he was blinded as a German although he was a Jew. Baum's fate he took as symbolic of the situation of the German-speaking Jews of Prague.

Assimilation into non-Jewish society had been impossible for the Jews in the Austro-Hungarian Empire before 1848; now it was legally possible, but this fact created not only problems of adaptation for the Jews but also resentment and fear among the Gentile majority. Germanized Jews played an important part in the life of Prague, they outnumbered the Germans and dominated its professions, but were distrusted and often hated by Czechs and Germans alike. Age-old religious and racial prejudices were inflamed by economic factors. Middle-class Czechs and Germans who had suffered from the economic expansion of the late nineteenth century resented the success of the Jews who owned much of the industry and commerce in Bohemia. In the 1880s German nationalistic feeling, linked with anti-Semitism, gained momentum in Austria, and nowhere was it stronger than in Bohemia. Czech nationalism had even deeper roots, and outbreaks of violence were common. In this unfortunate environment Kafka found it difficult to establish his own position and attitude. His father did not help him to identify with any group: according to the occasion he cursed Czechs, Germans, Jews, everyone except himself (H. 169).

In the search for assimilation the Kafka family had lost its religious faith and its sense of racial and cultural identity. Kafka knew that religion meant little to his father and his visits to the synagogue four times a year bored the boy. Religious instruction at school was quite

A class photograph of 1899. Top row, second from left, Kafka; third row, second from left, Oskar Pollak

meaningless to him. His Bar Mitzvah at the age of thirteen was to him a ludicrous ritual. The synagogue housed the relics of the Jewish martyr Solomon Molcho, yet in 1911 Kafka professed to be unfamiliar with that name. Only later was he to see his own insecurity as an essentially Jewish trait and to note that the Prague Jew suffered from a particularly acute feeling of homelessness.

At school Kafka was a good pupil, but weak in mathematics. He had an inordinate fear of examinations, always believing that the teachers would discover the 'truth' about his abilities – that he had none. Lessons scarcely interested him, for everything outside himself seemed of little substance. He later likened his attitude to school to the interest a defaulting bank clerk might show in the everyday business of the institution where he continues to work, fearful of discovery (H. 207). His grammar school concentrated on the classics – the hero of his novel *America* remarks that European schools rarely offered a useful education in modern languages and commercial subjects. Kafka's schoolmates, to most of whom he remained distant, believed him to be a conscientious pupil but one who was not interested in his studies. He himself saw his indifference as the sign of a bad pupil. There was little personal contact between teachers and pupils and the prescribed syllabus left little room to explore individual interests. At school, as in the family, Kafka felt that his individuality was rejected and that he was expected to conform to a pattern foreign to his nature. In response he tended to shut himself off from the world, afraid all the time that this world would suddenly catch up on him and notice his failure to respond to its demands. Although he would occasionally rebel against the attitudes of those who actually or apparently condemned him, his predominant reaction was to look for faults in himself which would explain the verdict of others. His isolation and anxiety increased.

Rejecting religion, Kafka turned in his last years at school to scientific materialism and atheism. Under the influence of one of his teachers he read with enthusiasm Darwin and the part-Darwinian philosopher of science Ernst Haeckel, whose *Riddle of the Universe* had just appeared. He took an interest in an anti-clerical society and engaged in discussions with a school-friend in which he liked to think that he disproved the existence of God. Another classmate introduced him at the age of sixteen to socialism. Usually timid, he wore a red carnation to school as a sign of his political sympathies. Kafka's interest in socialism arose, no doubt, from his sense of social justice and his longing for comradeship. The doctrine of international brotherhood probably appealed to him. All his class automatically became members of a German nationalist student organization, but Kafka was expelled for refusing to stand during the singing of *Die Wacht am Rhein*, a rallying song of German nationalism.

'Free gymnastic instruction for the sons of Bavarian working men', a snapshot in Munich's municipal playgrounds showing small boys engaged in physical drill

By the age of fourteen or fifteen Kafka had begun to write. He composed little plays which were acted by his young sisters in the family circle to mark their parents' birthdays. More ambitiously, he began to write a novel. His family had no feeling for such things, and when an uncle rejected his writing as 'the usual rubbish' Kafka withdrew still further into himself.

He had only a few friends and perhaps because of this cherished an ideal of friendship, a relationship of mutual understanding and support through which he might escape from his isolation and insecurity. Oskar Pollak, his closest friend in his last school years and his first year at university, was to him a link with the outside world, a window through which he could look on to the streets, as he put it (BR. 20). Through Pollak he developed an interest in the philosophy of Nietzsche and in a group of writers associated with the periodical *Kunstwart* who, inspired by Nietzsche, aimed to replace the decadent spirit of the late nineteenth century with a more vital culture. Kafka fell temporarily under the spell of the neo-Nietzschean language of 'depth' and 'folksiness', which was a desperate attempt to return to natural strength in art, not unconnected with the contemporary cults of open air, sun and water that were also not without fascination for him. He was, it seems, looking for a new vitalism, for values in life other than those of rationalism and science. Like Nietzsche, he saw himself as one chosen to suffer in life, but unlike that philosopher he envied rather than despised the ordinary man with his unquestioning acceptance of the world. He could not accept Nietzsche's dismissal of conventional morality, nor see himself as a superman. Yet Nietzsche's diagnosis of moral and cultural malaise, his scepticism, rejection of rationalism and middle-class values, and his emphasis on individuality had a profound effect on Kafka as on his whole generation. Kafka's sense of failure was no doubt aggravated by Nietzsche's glorification of the will-power that he felt he lacked.

In 1901, having passed his matriculation examination, Kafka enrolled in the German university of Prague. His own inclination was towards the arts, but he began by studying chemistry, no doubt in order to remain close to Pollak. After only two weeks he changed to law, a course which must have met with his father's approval since it would fit his son for a secure and socially acceptable career in the Austrian civil service. After a short time reading history and German, Kafka continued with law although he found it intensely boring; it was, he wrote, a process of eating sawdust which had already been masticated in a thousand mouths (H. 207).

Through literary and artistic societies at university Kafka became familiar with the work of fashionable contemporary authors. At a meeting of one such society a fellow student, Max Brod, gave a talk on Schopenhauer, and Kafka was drawn from his normal reticence to object to Brod's attack on Nietzsche.

From this encounter arose a friendship which was to last until Kafka's death. Kafka admired Brod, who was himself soon to become a successful author, as a man of energy who could cope with practical life and was able to write prolifically and with apparent ease. The two young men had in common a dissatisfaction with their studies, an antipathy towards the normal careers that awaited them and a desire to devote as much of their time as possible to creative writing. Their tastes in literature were, however, not identical. When Brod expressed his enthusiasm for purple passages from neo-romantic poets, Kafka quoted a simple phrase from Hugo von Hofmannsthal's *Gespräch über Gedichte* (*Dialogue on Poems*), 'the smell of damp flags in a hall', then remained silent as if these words spoke for themselves. By 1903 or 1904, when he came close to Brod and broke with Pollak, Kafka was disenchanted with the neo-Nietzschean style and was striving for a more sober manner. In this aim he diverged from the practice of most contemporary German writers, and particularly from that of other Prague authors who tended to react against the poverty of Prague German, its stilted bureaucratic syntax and limited vocabulary, by indulging in neo-romantic effusions of the poetic imagination. Yet Kafka could not find true inspiration and destroyed what he wrote. Nevertheless, during these first years at university, if not before, he began to think that he might justify himself by accepting his assumed peculiarity and becoming a creative writer.

Through Brod Kafka met the young aspiring artists and writers of Prague. Mostly he remained reserved and non-committal. They were too flamboyant, even in the knowledge of their own estrangement. One Sunday a group of poets paraded through the town, dressed in their tight-waisted suits, each with a red rose in his hand. Kafka disapproved of sensationalism. Yet because of their social alienation the poets of Prague, Brod, Paul Leppin, Gustav Meyrink, lived in a world of the imagination, flirting with mysticism, eroticism, and gruesome adventure, often inspired by local legend. It was a time of experiment and the flouting of convention, as neo-romanticism, art for art's sake,

Drawing of Max Brod by Willi Nowak

Marc Chagall *The Sabbath* 1910

decadence and decorative Art Nouveau gave way to the first signs
of Expressionism. Rilke, brought up in Prague, was influenced by this
hothouse atmosphere. Franz Werfel, another child of Prague, seven
years younger than Kafka, who was to become a leading Expressionist
poet, was a close associate of Brod's for several years. Brod, Werfel
and Kafka attended spiritualist séances together. Werfel's poetry expresses a longing for union with the cosmos and his fellow men, for a

new humanity based on love and humility; but he also wrote of despair, and his themes of guilt and redemption, self-accusation and ecstasy reflect a cultural dilemma. Kafka admired Werfel, but was not happy with the rhetorical bombast of his language, nor indeed with the loud style of Expressionist writing in general as it was to develop over the next two decades.

Brod himself, in these early years of his career, believed in Schopenhauer's doctrine that the artist should withdraw from the material exigencies of life in order to find a higher truth. He called his attitude 'indifferentism': the belief that, since judgement was impossible, everything in life was equally valid. He, too, had mystical tendencies, and like the other poets of Prague was fascinated by the sordid aspects of city life – drunks, prostitutes, murders and suicides. But Kafka could not bear even a dirty joke, and preferred writers who portrayed youth and innocence – Hesse and Carossa.

Kafka's aversion to bombast may be connected with his reading of Hofmannsthal's *Chandos Letter* of 1901, a now famous document of the poet's doubts about the ability of language to describe reality. Kafka's own doubts about the function of language were increased by the knowledge that his German, the German of Prague, was an isolated, even artificial tongue, not true German or the language of a true community.

He spent much time on his own, reading biographies, diaries and letters of famous writers – Goethe, Grillparzer, Byron, Schopenhauer, Hebbel, Dostoyevsky. Evidently he was looking for those experiences of other men in some way similar to himself which might illuminate his personal situation and help him to piece together a consistent view of life. He tended to distrust abstract philosophy and to look to empirical sources for the answers to his problems. He had an especial interest in those poets and authors who had been alienated from society and whose genius had brought them suffering. Generalizing from his own experience Kafka inclined to accept the Romantic concept of the artist as an ill-starred outsider, together with the proposition, basic to the thought of both Schopenhauer and Nietzsche, that suffering was an essential part of existence and the means to true wisdom.

In his second term at university Kafka had attended lectures on philosophy given by Anton Marty, a pupil of the eminent philosopher Franz Brentano. In the following years he occasionally took part in the discussions of a small group of followers of Brentano who met in the Café Louvre in Prague. From the Louvre circle he moved on to intimate gatherings organized by Berta Fanta, a chemist's wife. Here discussion ranged over philosophical problems, Kant, Fichte, Hegel, and recent discoveries, Planck's quantum theory, and Einstein's theory of relativity. Kafka was not normally receptive to abstract ideas, but Brentano's theories were supposedly empirical and this may have impressed him. Franz Brentano, now best known for his influence on psychology and on Husserl's phenomenology, had in his *Psychology from an empirical standpoint* of 1874 denied that man can have direct knowledge of the external world, a point which must have strengthened Kafka's basic uncertainty about reality and which he could find expressed in the work of one of his favourite authors, Heinrich von Kleist. According to Brentano only the perception of one's own mental acts is not subject to error, and he therefore stressed the importance of rigorous self-analysis. This argument may have encouraged Kafka's tendency to look into himself for truth and certainty. Of the three types of mental act defined by Brentano, representation, emotional reaction and judgement, only the last was held by him to be a sure basis of moral behaviour. Whether, however, Brentano's 'judgement' was for Kafka linked with the judgements, judicial processes, and questions of guilt which occur in his writings from 1912 onwards remains problematical. Clearly, however, he had not rejected reason as a means to knowledge.

Kafka had other interests during his student years. One was the theatre. He was a regular visitor to the German and Czech theatres in Prague and much enjoyed the lowbrow entertainment offered by the city's *cafés chantants*. He was fascinated by those amusements which could raise man above the pains of existence. In his liking for the country and country-folk we can see his worship of what seemed to him the normal and natural aspects of life. Similar longing for communion with nature, and an interest in primitivism, as antidotes to social and cultural malaise, are reflected in the art and literature of his contemporaries. He spent several vacations in the country, often with his uncle Siegfried, went on long walks alone or with friends, and was a keen swimmer and rower. The vegetarian diet which he observed for long periods, his dislike of coffee and tea, and his tendency to place faith in nature-cures sprang from his longing for health and naturalness. He felt that his general lack of health, which in these early adult years showed itself in headaches, constipation and a feeling of debility, was a result of his inability to cope with life mentally, and indeed some of his ills were probably psychosomatic. Himself a thin man, he connected leanness with frailty and lack of fitness to withstand life, and was always ready to place confidence in men of solid build or imposing rotundity.

During his student years he may have lost some of his timidity and social gaucheness, but he remained basically retiring and introspective. Conscious of his 'abnormality' and of his desire to write, he was searching for a philosophy of life which would explain both his inner state and outer reality and which he might proclaim in his writing. Success as a writer might justify his life to himself and to the world. A later recollection of this longing probably refers to these student days: 'I went over the wishes that I wanted to realize in life. I found that the most important or the most delightful was the wish to attain a view of life (and – this was necessarily bound up with it – to convince others of it in writing), in which life, while still retaining its natural full-bodied rise and fall, would simultaneously be recognized no less clearly as a nothing, a dream, a dim hovering' (BK. 281). In 1920 he commented that this was an impossible wish, or at least felt and expressed wrongly, since it was a form of self-defence, an attempt to justify not only the world but also his existence in it.

It was probably while at university, in 1904 or 1905, that Kafka wrote *Beschreibung eines Kampfes* (*Description of a Struggle*), the earliest of his works to have been preserved. Parts of this work were published in the periodical *Hyperion* in 1908 and 1909. In neither of its versions does it express an all-embracing and all-explaining view of life, but presents a collection of scenes and dialogues as dreams rather than as reality.

The narrator's unashamedly selfish desire for friendship seems to reflect Kafka's own longing. He makes himself look foolish in his concern not to offend his companion in any conceivable way: he bends double as he walks lest his height disturb the other man. He sees in him someone whose possible respect will give him the sense of importance he desires: 'From these words I imagined that my acquaintance suspected in me something which, although it wasn't there, made me nevertheless rise in his estimation. . . . Who knows, this man . . . might be capable of bestowing on me in the eyes of the world a value . . .' (BK. 17). When the acquaintance seems to want to be left alone the narrator runs away in terror and decides to withdraw into himself in order to avoid hurt and preserve his dignity. The attempt to establish contact with the other man arouses extreme and conflicting emotions in himself, an obsequious desire to please, a fear of being hurt and even destroyed, and a longing to dominate.

Marc Chagall *The Poet Reclining* 1915

Later the narrator is alone in the countryside, or in a dream land-
scape that he creates for himself: 'Here I could be content. For here it
is secluded and beautiful. . . . Thus I toyed with my future life and
tried stubbornly to forget.' (BK. 31) He presses his face to the ground;
it is too much effort to register this reality, an unstable and absurd
world which reduces him to a state of anguished hopelessness.

Alfred Kubin *The Spider* 1902

Erich Heckel *Reading Aloud* 1914

Stranger still is a scene in which he sees an obese oriental carried on a litter by four naked men. The Far East was a subject of general interest at the time Kafka wrote this story, not long after the Boxer rebellion: in 1903 a Prague artist, Emil Orlik, had done some Japanese scenes, in 1904 the Expressionist painters Kirchner and Heckel 'discovered' the Japanese woodcut, and Kafka himself was impressed by translations of Chinese poetry. This may help to explain why the narrator hopes to learn from this oriental 'something about the dangers of this apparently safe country'. Before the fat man is drowned in the river he attempts to ford, he relates a long conversation with 'the man who prayed'. The latter suffers from seasickness on land and seems to convince the oriental of 'the impossibility of living' (the subtitle of this section of the work). He thinks even his own body insubstantial and beyond his control. Kafka experienced a similar dissociation of mind and body when he wrote that his own arm muscles seemed very far from him (T. 21.2.'11). The 'man who prayed' relates a simple extract

27

from everyday normality which worries him since he cannot understand how others can accept reality without amazement or bewilderment. The same episode had been recorded by Kafka in a letter to
Max Brod in 1904 (BR. 29):

> When as a small child I opened my eyes after a brief afternoon nap, still
> not quite sure I was alive, I heard my mother up on the balcony asking in
> a natural tone of voice: 'What are you doing, my dear? Goodness, isn't
> it hot?' From the garden a woman answered: 'Me, I'm having my tea
> on the lawn.'

Kafka had commented that he was amazed at the steadfastness with
which people could bear life.

As in many of Kafka's later works there is no clear dividing line
between reality and fantasy, and the characters, who change attitudes
in a bewildering manner, are suspiciously like projections of the
narrator's imagination. In the struggle between the person who flees
reality and the one who appears to be at home in the world we can
see those two possibilities of action which Kafka believed were open
to him. Here both are shown to be equally uncertain of success. As
in Kafka's later work, the characters are functions rather than personal-
ities, and the women exist in the minds of the men as promises of
security. In *Das Urteil* (*The Judgement*) father and son seem more sub-
stantial but change roles much as the narrator and the acquaintance do
here. *Description of a Struggle* is lacking in connection and conviction;
nor does its style have the sobriety and control evident in Kafka's more
successful stories. Perhaps this story renders life as 'a nothing, a dream,
a floating', but it fails to capture its 'natural weighty rise and fall'.
Nevertheless, like most first works, it reveals a great deal of the
author's personality and throws considerable light on his major writings.

Kafka took his doctorate in law in the shortest possible time, after five
years at the university. He had called upon all his reserves of energy and
determination in order to complete his studies and be independent of
his father. But he was still undecided about his future. In the autumn
of 1906, at the age of twenty-three, he began work as an unpaid trainee
in the law courts for a year, a prerequisite for a career at the Bar. He
hoped to find a position which would give him financial independence
and allow him free time in which to write.

Hochzeitsvorbereitungen auf dem Lande (*Wedding Preparations in the
Country*), probably written in 1907, is quite different in tone from

Description of a Struggle. Kafka was still searching for his true manner. It is the beginning of a novel in which Eduard Raban (German *Raabe* – raven, not far removed from Czech *kavka*) leaves the town where he lives and works to visit his fiancée in the country. It is possible that the relationship of Raban and his fiancée was to be an imaginative development of Kafka's emotional involvement with an older woman in a sanatorium in Zuckmantel, Silesia, where he had spent a few weeks in 1905 and 1906 recovering from the strain imposed on his health by hard study. Raban suffers from anxieties and a lack of confidence similar to those of the narrator and the 'worshipper' of the earlier work. He wishes he could stay at home and simply send his body on the journey; his incorporeal self would then curl up in bed in the shape of a beetle. This thought was later to be taken up in *Die Verwandlung* (*The Metamorphosis*). Raban's feelings remain within comprehensible bounds and the fragment is noteworthy for the detached realistic or impressionistic descriptions of the street and the train journey. Yet the outside world is, it seems, a reflection of the hero's dampened soul – rain and darkness dominate. If he aimed to capture the meaning of reality then Kafka failed, for reality escaped his grasp, or rather ceased to be real as soon as it was rendered into words. Kafka was ever conscious of this problem which he seems to describe in a sketch written in 1920 called *Der Kreisel* (*The Top*). There he portrays the frustration of a man who wishes to understand the spinning top: every time he seizes the moving object it becomes dead in his hands.

In October 1907 Kafka accepted a humble post in an insurance company in the hope of eventually being sent abroad. Many times in his life he was to dream of escaping from Prague. He felt that the city was a monster that suffocated him, yet it fascinated him too. It seemed to him

Alfred Kubin *Bad Dream c.* 1900

Premises of the insurance company of the Wenzelsplatz where Kafka worked 1907–1908. Photograph on a postcard sent to Max Brod 1910

to have an uncanny, almost demonic power; its history contained strong occult elements, and this background may help to explain not only his inability to tear himself away from the town but also the fascination with the grotesque evident in so many of his works. The urban setting of his stories owes much to the nocturnal aspect of the old city, strange, labyrinthine, moribund, even ghostly. To the German Jew who felt uneasy outside its limits, in the Czech environment of the new town or the surrounding countryside, it was, despite its glories of Gothic and Baroque architecture, a claustrophobic place; and many of its young artists left at the first opportunity. But now he worked in his office from eight until six and was required to put in unpaid over-time, even on Sundays. He complained of exhaustion in the evenings and of being deadened by office routine; after only a few days with the company he wrote that he might gradually turn into wood, from the finger-tips upward (BR. 49). He found that he had no opportunity for creative writing and started to look for another job.

The following year he found a job with an industrial accident insur-ance company which was to suit him a little better and in which he remained for fourteen years. Here, in the *Arbeiter-Unfalls-Versicherungs-Anstalt für das Königreich Böhmen*, he worked only from eight until two. As a Jew he was fortunate to get such a job in a semi-Government institution. He was appreciated by his subordinates as a kindly and understanding man and by his superiors as a person of intelligence who could be trusted and was particularly gifted at drawing up reports. He was concerned with the legal side of insurance and with classifying factories and workshops according to their degree of accident risk. He was required to travel throughout Northern Bohemia in order to inspect factory premises. The faults of bureaucracy, the red tape, the slow channels of communication and the apparently distant and unapproachable majesty of the highest authorities, as reflected in *Der Prozess* (*The Trial*) and *Das Schloss* (*The Castle*), were all experienced by Kafka. He observed how men who had claims against the company approached its officials in an attitude of subservience, making humble petitions rather than demanding rights: blind acceptance of authority was later to be delineated in the secondary characters in his two great novels. At first he hoped to be instrumental in improving working conditions in Bohemia. Alfred Weber, Max Weber's younger brother, later known as one of the leading social scientists of his age, taught at the university; perhaps through his teaching, as well as through his own interest in socialist ideas, Kafka was aware of the suffering caused by industrial and bureaucratic systems which he now observed at first hand. He drew up plans for improving the safety of machines but found that employers were seldom interested and the workers themselves apathetic. Reforms were slow to be put into practice. Gradually disillusioned with his work, Kafka became increasingly convinced that it was stifling his creative energies and deadening his soul. Yet he would not prostitute his talents (as he saw it) by entering on a career as a journalist. His basic insecurity did not allow him to do more than contemplate drastic solutions to his problems, and he tended to prefer the present situation to an untried alternative. He remained with the company, but even promotion did not convince him that he was good at his job, since his heart was not in it.

From 1908 to 1912 Kafka's interest in left-wing politics increased. He attended meetings addressed by leading Czech political figures and went to the *Klub Mladych* (Young People's Club), a revolutionary socialist organization. (Unlike most of the German-speaking Jews of Prague, he had a fluent command of the Czech language and did not isolate himself from the Czech community altogether.) In 1912 the *Klub Mladych* was declared illegal. When police broke up its last meeting, called to protest against the execution of the trades union leader Liabeuf in Paris, Kafka was, according to one, disputed, report, arrested for refusing to leave the hall, but released after paying a fine.

A manuscript page from Kafka's *Diaries*

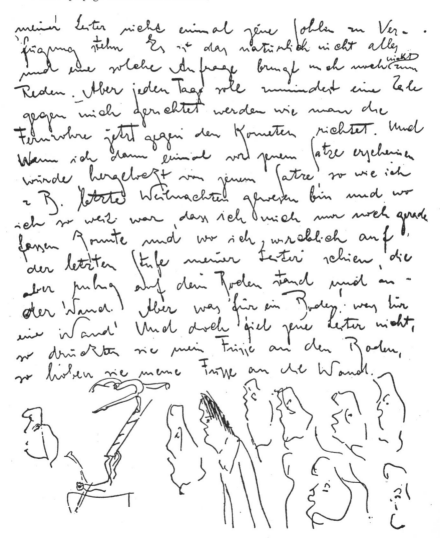

Sketch from Kafka's *Diaries*

In his diary we find cryptic entries which record his reading of socialist and communist literature. He met exiled Russian revolutionaries and followed with interest the Chaluz movement in Palestine which put into practice some of the theories of the Russian revolutionaries of 1905. In Czech socialist circles he met Jaroslav Hašek, who was later to write *The good soldier Schweik* and whose humour and disrespect for authority appealed to Kafka. A more reputable politician, respected by Kafka and Brod, was Thomas Masaryk, who became president of the Czech republic after 1918.

In 1910 Kafka began to keep a diary or notebook in which he recorded his emotional states and wrote down sketches and ideas for stories. He was severely critical of his own meagre output. Max Brod prevented him from retiring into his shell completely and introduced him to two men who became his friends, the philosopher and Zionist Felix Weltsch and the blind author Oskar Baum. Brod constantly urged Kafka to write and to publish, but with little success. He suggested that they should together write a novel to be called *Richard und Samuel*, a venture that did not progress beyond a few pages. He took Kafka to cafés and nightclubs and they made several journeys together, to Riva on Lake Garda in 1909, to Paris in 1910, to Italy and Paris in 1911, and to Weimar, the home of German classical literature, in 1912.

After this last trip Kafka stayed for a few days in the Harz mountains, at an establishment devoted to nature therapy. His diary for this period reflects a strange mixture of irony and respect for the cults of vegetarianism, gymnastics, nudism and the open air. At first he was distinguished from the others at the morning exercises by the trunks he wore; later he lost some of his inhibitions, but found the sight of naked flesh often anything but inspiring: 'When I see these stark-naked people moving slowly past the trees (though they are usually at a distance), I now and then get light, superficial attacks of nausea. . . . Old men who leap naked over haystacks are no particular delight to me either' (T. 11.7.'12).

Kafka was pursuing other interests independently of Brod. In 1911 he visited the father of anthroposophy, Rudolf Steiner, and showed interest in his ideas, hoping rather half-heartedly to discover a faith which would answer his longing for certainty about the meaning of life. By now he seems to have been convinced that his yearnings would never be satisfied and was not surprised to find Steiner a disappointment as a man. On this occasion Kafka exercised his keen eye for human failings in others as well as in himself.

But it was Max Brod who first took him to plays performed by a troupe of eastern European Jews in Prague in 1910. The fascination the Yiddish theatre exercised on Kafka is attested by the entries in his diaries. In 1911 he befriended the actor Jizchak Löwy, a Jew from Poland who played leading roles in the Yiddish plays. Although he knew little or no Yiddish Kafka was entranced by the performances and felt a natural sympathy for the language. He organized and introduced entertainments starring Löwy and began to study the history of Jewish literature and to learn Hebrew. The Yiddish actors were ignored and despised as social outcasts by assimilated German Jews in Prague, and Kafka's father disapproved strongly of his association with Löwy – 'My father about him: "Whoever lies down with dogs gets up with fleas" ' (T.3.11.'11). Kafka now heard of the pogroms in Russia and recognized more poignantly than before the hopelessness of the Jewish situation and the courage of the people who retained a sense of humour amid disaster. He now saw that his personal predicament could be linked with that of the Jewish race. The Jews of eastern Europe had suffered con-tinual persecution and had not been allowed to become assimilated into their cultural environment. For them their religion was not just a meaningless tradition as Kafka felt it had become among the western Jews. The Hassidism of the eastern Jews, with its rejection of rabbinical exclusiveness and intellectualism, its emphasis on moral standards, religious consecration and the joy of living, and particularly its appeal to the suffering poor, made a great impre ion on him. Above all, like Brod and Martin Buber (who spoke in Prague in 1909), he saw in Hassidism a movement which at its best seemed to be able to produce a sense of community in faith. It is possible that his later work was in-fluenced by Hassidic ideas, the belief in the immanence of God in all existence, the interrelationship of heaven and earth and the cosmic significance of all human actions. The wondrous events of Jewish parables and the surrealism of the Yiddish theatre also probably had an effect on his creative imagination.

Flora Klug 'who imitated gentlemen', an actress in the Yiddish theatre

Shortly after the Yiddish troupe left Prague Kafka began attending Zionist meetings. The intolerable position of the eastern Jews after they had been made scapegoats for the abortive revolution of 1905 had brought new meaning to the age-old aspirations for a return to Israel. Max Brod was converted to Zionism at this time and became one of its leading champions. He began to write of man's relationship with God and of the hope that lay in divine goodness in man. A temporary estrangement of the friends occurred when Kafka remained sceptical of Zionism. He seems to have felt that the Jewish problem could not be solved by thinking in terms of a nation state.

Kafka had several sketches and stories in manuscript and had published a few of these in periodicals. In 1912 he was finally persuaded by Brod and by the publisher Kurt Wolff to collect some of this material into a book. Various sketches or prose poems, written between 1904 and early 1912, appeared under the title *Betrachtung* (*Meditation*) late in 1912. Some of the pieces were taken from the two earlier works discussed above, some are adapted from entries in his diary with the more obviously personal elements removed. The volume contains impressionistic recordings of apparently insignificant events and fanciful dreamlike sequences. Exceptionally large print compensated for the slightness of the sketches. The themes are similar to those of *Description of a Struggle*: anxiety, uncertainty, search for release and isolation or for companionship, amazement at the unquestioning attitude of others. Another theme which reflected the author's thoughts, the association of the bachelor with isolation and unhappiness, is found in the sketch called *Das Unglück des Junggesellen* (*The Bachelor's Misfortune*) written in November 1911. First recorded in his diary, this piece shows Kafka's deep longing for companionship in marriage and his desire to assume family responsibilities and thereby find integration into society. For he was now approaching thirty years of age, generally taken as a decisive point in life; at this age his father had founded his family.

Kafka's early publications did not make a literary stir. Weird stories were common enough and his did not strike an obviously new note. In his review of *Meditation* Brod felt obliged to deny the clear similarity between Kafka's work and the writings of the then well-known Robert Walser. Another reviewer pointed to the affinity between Kafka and Alfred Kubin, the graphic artist and novelist who lived in Prague. Kubin, in his mixture of fantasy and realism, humour and horror, offers a visual counterpart to aspects of Kafka's work. Kafka bought ten copies of *Meditation* from a Prague bookshop and wondered what happened to the one copy that remained in stock. The pieces he wrote before 1912 are now of interest mainly for the light they throw on his attitude to reality and on his later work.

Alfred Kubin *Fever Tapestry c.* 1920

1912 overtures

On the evening of 13 August 1912 Kafka went to Brod's home to go over the manuscript of *Meditation* with him and there met the woman to whom he was to be officially engaged twice – in 1914 and 1917. His relationship with her caused him more emotional conflict than anything else in his life, including his father-complex and the conflict between writing and office work. Indeed his feelings for Felice Bauer and the question of marriage brought all his other problems to a crisis. In the *Letter to My Father* he wrote that his abortive attempts to reach the haven of marriage had called forth a struggle between all the positive forces he could muster and a furious army that formed a barrier between himself and marriage – an army of 'all the negative forces that I have described as being the result in part of your method of upbringing, that is to say, the weakness, the lack of self-confidence, the sense of guilt' (H. 208). The year of 1912 was a turning-point in Kafka's life and in his literary career.

Max Brod and Kafka showed Felice Bauer some photographs taken on their trip to Weimar a few weeks before. Kafka seems to have been attracted to the girl immediately, although he tried to maintain his detachment by describing her dispassionately in his diary:

> Miss F.B. When I arrived at Brod's on 13 August she was sitting at the table. I was not at all curious about who she was, but rather took her for granted at once. Bony, empty face that wore its emptiness openly.

> Bare throat. A blouse thrown on. Looked very domestic in her dress although, as I later discovered, she by no means was. (I alienate myself from her a little by inspecting her so closely. What a state I'm in now, indeed, alienated in general from the whole of everything good, and don't even believe it yet . . .) Almost broken nose. Blonde, rather straight, unattractive hair, strong chin. As I was taking my seat I looked at her closely for the first time, by the time I was seated I already had an unshakeable opinion. (T. 20.8. '12)

The good that he saw in her was partly the energy and ability to cope with life that he admired in anyone, and partly the prospect of a relationship which might bring true companionship and support. At this first meeting she seemed willing to accompany him on a visit to Palestine; the apparent ease with which she made this decision impressed him. Furthermore she seemed to be close to him through her experience of suffering as a child, her lack of enthusiasm for food, her interest in literature and her habit of reading through the night. Kafka was doubtless feeling rather buoyant: he was about to appear in print, he felt at home in the Brod family where the parents were proud of their son and welcomed his friends, and he had been excited by a brief and superficial relationship with a girl in Weimar.

Marriage was to Kafka an ideal for which he longed but which he suspected was beyond his reach. In November 1911 he had become involved against his own wish in the management of a factory which was part of his family's expanding business interests. On the improbable occasion of a visit to a lawyer to discuss the allocation of shares in the factory Kafka's longing for marriage and children made itself felt:

> When the lawyer, in reading the agreement to me, came to a passage concerning my possible future wife and possible children, I saw across from me a table with two large chairs and a smaller one around it. At the thought that I should never be in a position to seat in these or any other three chairs myself, my wife, and my child, there came over me a yearning for this happiness so despairing from the very start that in my excitement I asked the lawyer the only question I had left after the long reading, which at once revealed my complete misunderstanding of a rather long section of the agreement that had just been read. (T. 8.11.'11)

From *A Bachelor's Misfortune* it appears that Kafka saw in marriage proof of a man's maturity not only to himself but also in the eyes of the world. To marry and become a father would be to free himself from his father and rid himself of his feelings of inferiority. It would mean finally and indubitably standing on his own feet and, what is more, accepting responsibility for others; it would be the greatest possible personal achievement: 'Marrying, founding a family, accepting all the children that come, supporting them in this insecure world and perhaps even guiding them a little, is, I am convinced, the utmost a human being can succeed in doing at all' (H. 209). Marriage would also direct sexual instincts into a socially and morally acceptable channel.

In common with Max Brod and most of the respectable sons of Prague Kafka had visited some of the numerous brothels that existed in the old city. The unwritten law of the time demanded experience of the young man as it demanded chastity of the well-bred young woman. Kafka himself was looking in his relations with whores for proof of his masculinity and for companionship. Such physical sex, however, only filled him with disgust. His sense of guilt was probably increased because the girls belonged to the exploited Czech nation. His earliest experience of sexual intercourse, with a shop girl in a cheap hotel, nauseated him, and he always associated sex with dirt and obscenity although he felt that the body had need of it: 'My body, sometimes quiet for years, would then again be shaken to the point of not being able to bear it by this desire for a small, a very specific abomination . . . even in the best that existed for me there was something of it, some small nasty smell, some sulphur, some hell' (BRM. 182). He had at least one quite serious affair, with a barmaid of whom he once said to Brod that whole cavalry regiments had ridden over her body. In 1908 he had written to Brod that he had felt such an urgent need to be touched in friendship that he had gone with a whore to a hotel. She was, he said, too old to feel melancholy, but was sad that men could not love her as they would a mistress. Neither she nor Kafka gained any comfort from their meeting (BR. 59).

Casual sex proved unsatisfactory. But did not marriage involve the same sordid business? In this fear lay one cause of Kafka's anxiety about marriage. He recorded how the sight of his parent's bed with the night-clothes laid out upon it filled him with disgust (T. 18.10.'16). Thinking of his relationship with Felice, he wrote: 'Coitus as punishment for the happiness of being together. Live as ascetically as possible, more ascetic-ally than a bachelor, that is the only possible way for me to endure marriage. But she?' (T. 14.8.'13) In his attitude to marriage and chastity we see a typical awareness of irreconcilably contradictory considerations: marriage provides morally acceptable sex, it is com-panionship and acceptance of responsibility, a proof of one's ability to come to terms with life; yet it is also an abandonment of complete purity and an involvement with another person which destroys one's independence and personal integrity. Once marriage was a distinct prospect, Kafka became acutely aware of the conflict between his desire for integration into society and his dreams of himself as a writer; for to him the artist, almost by definition, needed solitude and stood outside society. Those great writers who had come to terms with society were objects of veneration to him, but only very rarely could he imagine himself joining their august ranks. For success in just one sphere of activity seemed almost beyond the bounds of possibility.

At first it seemed that his feeling for Felice could inspire him to write. He was acutely aware of his slowness in writing and of his long sterile periods. He felt that a close relationship would bring a new life of happiness and creativity. After meeting her he delayed four weeks before acting; his characteristic fears made it difficult for him to make a decisive move. On 20 September 1912 he wrote the first letter to Felice in Berlin reminding her of her interest in the trip to Palestine, a journey which he long considered but never made. He wrote that there was a connection between his thoughts of her and his creative writing. Probably he felt that Felice expected him to fulfil his promise as a writer and wanted to prove himself to her. His mind was full of thoughts of a possible future with her and of ideas for stories. Two days after writing to Felice, in the night of 22–3 September 1912, he wrote *Das Urteil* (*The Judgement*) which begins as Georg Bendemann writes a letter to announce his engagement. From mid-September onwards Kafka adopted a routine which was to recur in his short periods of intense creativity. He worked in the office from eight to two, slept until half past seven, then went for a walk, alone or in company, returned for supper with his family, and then wrote from eleven until two or three in the morning. To write he needed solitude and silence, and silence was not easily obtained in the flat except when his family were asleep. His sensitivity to noise is reflected in a sketch (*Grosser Lärm*, cf T. 5.11.'11) in which the narrator is assailed by slamming doors, noises from the kitchen, the voices of his parents and sisters, and the cheeping of canaries.

Kafka's urge to write was at this time so compelling that he entertained serious thoughts of suicide in October 1912 when his father insisted that he should spend his afternoons in the factory belonging to the family. Brod had to alert Kafka's mother to the danger. Kafka now despised his earlier efforts and felt increasing frustration at not being able to devote all his time to writing. Even in the first months of his love for Felice Bauer he was already worried by the idea that was later to plague him, namely that to live with her (or with anyone) would make writing impossible since it would bring an end to his solitude and his irregular routine.

Felice Bauer was a typist, later a chief clerk, with a Berlin firm dealing in dictaphones. She was a middle-class Jewish girl with an interest in contemporary literature but little understanding for Kafka's work. After their first meeting he did not see her for seven months. Naturally she was not entirely satisfied to be wooed from a distance, by a spate of daily letters, and suggested a meeting in Berlin at Christmas 1912. The power of his pen may be judged from the fact that she continued to respond to his love even when he refused to go to Berlin, explaining that he needed all his spare time to write. It seems that he did not want to meet her again. He needed the security that she gave him, but security at a distance; in Berlin she was far enough away to be no embarrassment to him and need not be involved in his relationship with his family. There was a paradox in his attitude to the girl which arose from his chronic uncertainty about himself and reality. In his letters he requested details of her everyday life as if to assure himself that she really existed. He could never be sure that he was in love with a real person and that she could love him if she recognized him for what he really was. Rather than expose both of them to disappointment he postponed the meeting. Yet he was ruthlessly candid in describing his own personality to her. With his doubts about his fitness for normal life he constantly returned to the thought that he would never be able to marry. In November 1912 he informed Felice that he was not healthy enough for marriage and fatherhood (BRF. 88). Earlier in that month he wrote to end the correspondence and the relationship, saying that he could only make her unhappy, but never despatched the letter (BRF. 83 f.). In all seriousness he told her that his lean frame contained scarcely enough energy for the creative writing which had first claim on his strength (BRF. 65). His letters seemed designed to alienate her, yet were probably an attempt to be completely honest and reveal all his peculiarities. He feared that no woman could possibly love a man who had been rejected by his family and must be rejected by every normal person. He was constantly testing her reactions, wishing to destroy the dream if it were a dream, and yet afraid to lose her love and the possibility of real understanding and companionship.

As far as possible he kept his feelings from his parents. Felice became almost his only real contact with the outside world and she lived to a large extent in his imagination. More and more he withdrew into himself, saw less of his friends, went less and less to the theatre and concentrated on writing letters to her and awaiting literary inspiration. His correspondence with Felice is full of passion and longing, yet even when he had before him her assurances of love, and then most particularly, his joy was tempered by a fear that tragic disillusion awaited both of them. The incredible intensity of his emotion involved an acute awareness that his joy was too great to be true. Each day he waited for her letter with trepidation, thinking that he might well have alienated her by something he had written. His work at the office became unreal to him, yet he feared that such mundane business was more real than the ideal of love that he cherished.

The two stories that Kafka wrote during this early stage of his relationship with Felice Bauer reflect feelings of inferiority and guilt. Although in both the protagonist comes into conflict with his father and his family and his failings are seen in this context, the feeling of inadequacy that characterizes them must also mirror the author's sense of unworthiness in his relationship with Felice. A decade later he wrote that *The Judgement* marked a turning-point in his life; it was a breakthrough in his literary development and a sudden bursting forth of the *Angst* that was henceforth to plague him: 'Each sentence in this story, each word, each – if I may say so – music is connected with "fear". On this occasion the wound broke open for the first time during one long night' (BrM. 214).

The Judgement was written in eight hours of concentrated work. Kafka referred to its composition as if it were involuntary and claimed not to understand his own story. It was the first work with which he was to any extent pleased, probably because it was completed at one session.

The story begins as a young businessman, Georg Bendemann, has overcome his reluctance to inform a friend in St Petersburg of his engagement; he seems embarrassed and ashamed of his decision to marry. Although he rarely goes into his widowed father's room, he does so now to tell him that he has written the letter. Thus he appears to admit the importance of this letter and some connection between his father and his friend. The father shows signs of senility; although he has good reason to remember the friend, he questions and then denies his existence. He accuses Georg of hiding things from him. Georg sees his father as an old man in need of care, suggests that he should move into his own more pleasant room, and plans to take him into his household once he is married rather than leave him to live alone. Meanwhile he proceeds to put his father to bed, convinced that he is ailing. The father interprets this action differently: the son is assuming the superior role, taking over as head of family, and by covering him with the bedclothes he is, as it were, putting him out of sight and mind. The father now reasserts his authority and inspires awe. He stands on the bed, towering above Georg, one hand on the ceiling as if he were the giant Atlas supporting the world. The father declares that he knows all about the friend in Russia, that he has corresponded with him' and already told him of Georg's engagement. He disapproves of the engagement and accuses his son of living a self-centred life. The story which began quietly and realistically has now become dramatic and surrealistic. The father condemns his son to death by drowning and without question Georg rushes down the stairs, frightening the maid on the way, runs on to the bridge over the river in front of the house and drops into the water, crying out that he had always loved his parents.

The reader is perplexed by the importance of the friend in Russia, amused but disturbed by the confrontation of father and son, and bewildered and even horrified by the lack of relation between the verdict and the possible faults of the victim. The story flouts reason yet requires interpretation. A mad sequence of events and labyrinthine thoughts is related as if it were an everyday occurrence. The sober but dramatic presentation compels us to believe that this distorted and horrifying world is in some way true.

Kafka believed that the story revealed much about his personality, for he asked Felice to show it to her father so that he should learn as much as possible about his prospective son-in-law (BrF. 419). He pointed to the cryptographic connection between his own name and that of the hero without its suffix – Bende(mann) – and noted a more involved link between the fiancée's name, Frieda Brandenfeld, and that of Felice Bauer, as if these connections had not been consciously intended and were discovered only later (T. 11.2.'13). Kafka was in the habit of rushing headlong downstairs and frightening anyone coming up (BrF. 297). When' he wrote the story he lived in a house overlooking the river Vltava (Moldau). After his first letter to Felice he was almost certainly considering the prospect of marriage and his father's probable reaction. The father in the story has the inconsistency and tyrannical nature that Kafka saw in his own father, and there is little doubt that his feelings of guilt towards his father are reflected in the story. The friend in St Petersburg, who is associated with poverty, revolution and religious faith, probably owes something to Kafka's acquaintance with Jizchak Löwy.

The biographical links do not, however, go much further than this. The father in the story was evidently intended as an archetypal father figure, for when Kafka read *The Judgement* to his friends in the home of Felix Weltsch he was pleased that Weltsch's father, after praising the vividness of the tale, pointed to his own chair and said, 'I can see this father before me' (T. 11.2.'13). Nor is Georg Bendemann identical with the author. Far from being an artist aware of symbolic meanings, he fails to understand those of his father's remarks which make sense only on a secondary level. When the father denies the friend's existence and then a few minutes later claims that he is this friend's representative, his words are either nonsensical or they must mean that the friend does not exist for Georg because Georg does not treat him as a friend. If friendship involves frankness and trust then this is true. If Georg is to marry he must give up the ideals associated with this friend. This is perhaps implied by the fiancée who said that if he had such friends he ought not to have got engaged. Kafka wrote that the friend in Russia was what Georg and his father have in common (T. 11.2.'13); this somewhat unhelpful remark may indicate that one part of Georg's consciousness or conscience is identified with the friend and the father. Yet Georg's final words show that he does not feel the judgement to be entirely just. Indeed, whatever Georg's 'crime' is, it is not a crime normally punishable by death.

Various interpretations of the story in psychological terms are possible. Some aspects of the tale seem to invite a religious or metaphysical interpretation. It was written the day after the Jewish feast of Yom Kippur, a time when the sins of humanity were to be remembered. It may be that Georg accepts his father's judgement as if it were the judgement of God despite the father's obvious imperfections. The father says to Georg 'An innocent child, yes, that you were, truly, but still more truly have you been a devilish human being!', words which could be a comment on the general problem of good and evil in mankind.

The Judgement is ambiguous in many ways. It hesitates between tragedy and comedy. Many elements are ludicrous or absurd, for instance when the father in his Atlas-like pose on the bed raises his shirt-tails (in imitation of the fiancée luring his son) and reveals a war wound on his thigh. It is ironic that Georg drops to his death from the very bridge which at first seemed to symbolize a way to happiness. To attempt to define Georg's guilt (or his father's) is to become involved in a string of paradoxes. Has he insulted his friend or spared him distress by withholding information from him? Is he anxious to care for his father or to get rid of him? Is his proposed marriage a step towards maturity or an irresponsible reaction to a sexual urge? Egocentricity and concern for others, good and evil are inextricably mixed. Such seems the import of the story. Its hermetic quality is brought about largely by a narrative device that was to become characteristic of Kafka: the events are told almost entirely from the perspective of the principal character so that the reader shares his restricted knowledge and understanding.

Kafka believed that *The Judgement* contained an essential truth but that each reader would have to find it for himself, he was not sure what it was. When he had written the story his thoughts turned to Freud (T. 23.9.'12), not unnaturally, since it deals with the ambiguity of human feelings and a love–hate relationship between father and son. But to look for more precise connections with Freudian psychology is not very helpful. Brod reports that Kafka found Freud's theories crude. Kafka indeed was suspicious of any theory that claimed to explain everything and was perhaps even more aware of the complexity of life than Freud.

The conflict between father and son was a theme common in German Expressionist writings, many of which also have a surrealistic quality similar to Kafka's. The Expressionists, rebelling against the materialism and commercialization of society, portrayed the younger generation embracing a spiritual, socialist, pacifist and humanitarian creed, defying their fathers and rejecting the aggressive imperialism of the age. Kafka respected, even feared that which he associated with the father and did not visualize a new generation founding a new society. Georg is not fighting for spiritual or human values, rather these are connected with the father and the friend. Kafka's representation of the father–son conflict is more pessimistic and more complex than that found in the idealistic visions of the German Expressionist writers. Their heroes often promise to redeem mankind through their suffering, but Kafka's figures cannot even help themselves. Yet the intensely personal character of his work links it with Expressionist poetry before 1914, and his visionary distortion of normal reality is characteristic of the art of that movement, which coincided with the period of his mature writing. In particular Munch's hallucinatory paintings, which had a decisive

Edvard Munch *The Scream* 1893

influence on German Expressionist art, are often strikingly similar in mood to Kafka's work.

Die Verwandlung (*The Metamorphosis*) was written in three weeks during November and December 1912. Kafka was dissatisfied with the final episode after the death of the hero. The happiness of the family after the son's death forms an obvious contrast with the rest of the story and the narrator is forced in these last paragraphs to abandon the perspective of the hero. Most readers do not, however, regard this as a serious weakness. Rather they are shaken by a story that is horrid, even disgusting, and incredible, yet at the same time convincing, fascinating and moving. Once the initial metamorphosis of Gregor Samsa into a bug is accepted, the actions of the characters, even when they are caricatures, proceed comprehensibly.

Gregor, a travelling salesman who dislikes his job and stays in it only to pay off his family's debt to his employer, wakes up one morning to find that his shape is no longer human. At the end of the story his dead body is swept up by the maid. During the few months he lives as an insect in his room he is an increasing embarrassment to his family, and the attitudes of his father, mother and sister change from a mixture of pity and disgust to hatred. On the three occasions he emerges from his room to establish contact with the family he is driven back by his father protecting the family against a supposed attack. Gregor can understand human speech but not make himself understood.

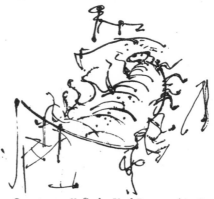

The Metamorphosis from *Drawings to Kafka* by Yosl Bergnes 'As Gregor Samsa awoke one morning from uneasy dreams he found himself transformed in his bed into a gigantic insect.'

The name Samsa (Czech *sämsa* – lonely) has similarities with Kafka. The writer admitted that the story was an indiscretion though not a confession (J. 55). Kafka spent much time lying on his back, suffering from migraine and symptoms of exhaustion or merely dreaming. The idea for *The Metamorphosis* occurred to him when he was lying in bed (BrF. 102). He must often have felt like a parasite, an object of resentment or disgust in his own family. Often, lacking vitality or inspiration, he would lie on the floor, good only to be swept up, as he wrote to Felice (BrF. 65).

But *The Metamorphosis* is not an autobiographical work. It is interesting as a dramatic story and as a comment on human relationships and communication. The matter-of-fact narration underlines the grotesqueness and the black humour of the tragic situation. The passage of time, the weather, the growing filth of Gregor's room and of his body are connected with his state of mind; the interrelation of inner and outer worlds is developed with such consistency that the latter seems hardly more than a projection of the hero's mind. This technique is, indeed, characteristic of much of Kafka's work. In *The Judgement* the physical appearance of the rooms and of the father mirrors Gregor's thoughts and feelings. In *The Trial* the process of relating everything to the hero's mental condition and narrating it from his perspective is so consistent that it is almost possible that everything happens in his mind, that he creates the story just as the narrator conjures up the natural scenery in *Description of a Struggle*.

Gregor's metamorphosis is incomprehensible to the characters in the story and to the reader. It is a blow that strikes as unexpectedly and inexplicably as fate in a Greek tragedy. Gregor's physical appearance remains somewhat vague. Apparently symbolic details are ambiguous. When the father drives Gregor back into his room by throwing apples at him, and one apple remains lodged in his back to cause a festering wound, are we to think of the tree of knowledge? Or is the throwing of apples connected with the same motif in Greek mythology, where it occurs in love-play? If either or both associations are valid, a peculiar perversion of myth has taken place. This is not improbable, for later stories (notably *The Silence of the Sirens* and *A Country Doctor*) involve a reinterpretation of myth or legend. *The Metamorphosis* itself has been called an anti-fairy-tale.

The story contains implied social criticism. The Samsa family is caught up in a world where money is all important. The firm in which Gregor works is impersonal and soul-destroying, yet his contacts with the boss are personal and embarrassing. The chief clerk who comes to check on Gregor's absence from work is a functionary who does not dare to exhibit a will of his own. All the characters operate as functions, not, however, primarily of a social system, but of the hero's situation.

There is also a hint of a metaphysical meaning. Gregor the bug at first eats rotting scraps, then loses all appetite. He longs for an unknown nourishment, and when he emerges from his room for the last time, attracted by his sister's violin playing, the music seems to point a way to this desired food. Apparently incestuous desires arise in Gregor, but his longing may be for something spiritual. Through art he might perhaps have found the satisfaction that is denied him. According to the Romantic tradition well-known to Kafka and embraced by him in his more hopeful moments in at least this one respect, art and more particularly music could give expression to the meaning of existence. Gregor perhaps realizes, however impurely and unclearly, what he lacks. It may be this lack of spiritual aim which has reduced him to a subhuman state.

The metamorphosis of Gregor Samsa reveals a paradox. If it results from his desire to escape from his enslavement to his job and from his responsibility towards his family, it brings enslavement of a more terrible kind. The 'metamorphosis' in his sister's attitude points to the paradoxical nature of love which so easily turns to hatred. Ambiguity is contained in details, for example in the words of the chief clerk: 'The chief did hint to me early this morning a possible explanation for your disappearance – with reference to the cash payments that were entrusted to you recently – but I almost pledged my solemn word of honour that this could not be so.' This equivocation may be comic to the uninvolved reader, but to Gregor it is hurtful. The absurdity of the metamorphosis itself is at once tragic and comic. No ordinary concepts of guilt and innocence suffice to explain Gregor's fate. As in *The Judgement*, guilt is connected with an inability to comprehend and to come to terms with the complexity and absurdity of life.

Unlike the characters of *Description of a Struggle* who expect the absurd, Bendemann and Samsa are confounded by it. The reader of *The Judgement* and *The Metamorphosis* is likewise confounded. In these two stories Kafka first gave compelling and dramatic expression to that perplexingly absurd yet strangely convincing world which was to become irrevocably linked with his name.

The idea for the novel *America* may have been in Kafka's mind for some time; a first (lost) version was composed early in 1912; but the bulk of the work, six chapters, was written in six weeks during September and October 1912, after *The Judgement* and before *The Metamorphosis*. In January 1913, after completing one more chapter, he abandoned the novel, only in 1914 to add a few more pages and what is probably the final but unfinished chapter. He published only its first chapter as a self-contained story entitled *The Stoker* and the rest of the unfinished work would have been lost to posterity but for Max Brod.

The novel tells of the fortunes of Karl Rossmann, a sixteen year old who has been sent to America by his parents after his seduction by the family maid in Prague. On arrival in New York he is unexpectedly welcomed by a rich uncle, but after a brief introduction to the world of big business he is rejected by his uncle, sets out across the country in the company of two tramps in search of work and fortune, takes employment as a lift-boy in an hotel, leaves this job in disgrace and becomes an unwilling servant to an ex-opera-singer, Brunelda. In the last chapter Karl is taken on as an employee by a mysterious theatre based in Oklahoma. If we ignore this puzzling last episode, Karl's progress takes him further and further down the social scale. One fragment sees him moving with Brunelda into an establishment that appears to be a brothel. Repeatedly he is condemned and rejected by those to whom he is responsible or on whom he depends: his father, his uncle, the head-waiter at the hotel. In each case he is seduced into transgression, by the maid, by a promised meeting with a millionaire's daughter, and by the tramp Robinson. Each time Karl feels that he is innocent and unjustly treated. In these recurring situations the person giving judgement is more concerned with discipline than with justice.

The distinction between justice and discipline is made by Karl's uncle in the first chapter. Arriving in New York harbour, Karl takes it upon himself to support a ship's stoker who claims that he has been unjustly dismissed. He believes passionately in his innocence without pausing to ask why. Yet he quite meekly follows his uncle and abandons the stoker when it is plain that the ship's captain will uphold the decision to dismiss him. His vacillation in intention and attitude to others is matched by that of the millionaire's wilful daughter Klara Pollunder. Karl is invariably so harassed that he scarcely questions sudden changes in others. Indeed, as the story is told from his perspective, the attitudes of the other characters reflect his expectations. The strange shifts in the characters correspond to changes in the hero's mood due, largely, to his immaturity.

Incomprehensible things happen to Karl Rossmann. Yet they turn out to be credibly motivated once certain information has been revealed. The impression of an irrational world results to a great extent from Karl's ignorance and inexperience. In this important respect the novel differs from *The Judgement* and *The Metamorphosis* in which the absurd remains unexplained. The apparently unbreakable spirit of the young hero and his ineradicable hope also give the novel an optimistic tone which is yet belied by his decline in fortune. Karl's goodness, his guilelessness and sense of loyalty are apparently unassailable, and he claims the reader's sympathy on moral grounds, a feature not found in Kafka's other heroes.

Although Kafka relied entirely on second-hand information he gives a credible impression of America, its size, the ceaseless activity of its people and the impact of technology on their lives. Yet this America does not differ greatly from the Europe he knew. The novel's title might therefore seem inappropriate, and indeed the other title that Kafka considered, *Der Verschollene* (*The Man who Disappeared*), seems more apt, as it sums up the hero's fate. Kafka called this work an imitation of Dickens, and although this statement is ultimately misleading, the story of a young man fighting his way alone and retaining his basic innocence in an unfriendly world has similarities with *David Copperfield* and *Oliver Twist*. The elements of social criticism are unmistakable. There is a clear contrast between the opulence of the rich and the extreme poverty and suffering of the workers. Karl becomes attached to an orphan girl whose mother died in circumstances reminiscent of the most lurid and most moving depictions of the sufferings of the poor in Dickens or Zola. The girl's report of her mother's death belongs to the great literary indictments of working-class conditions. Yet the contrast between the rich industrialists and bankers and the labouring masses, strikers and unemployed is not a major consideration in the mind of the hero. He remains faithful to middle-class values and does not give credence to attacks on the business methods of his uncle and his circle. He is more immediately impressed by the reduction of the worker to an automaton in a society ruled by machines. He sees men performing repetitive and unsatisfying jobs tied to the telephone and telegraph system. He also experiences the humiliation and degradation of an inferior in a hierarchical organization and the high-handedness of petty authority. Yet he accepts all this as a part of the world in which he must make his way, and only what appears to him to constitute blatant misuse of authority arouses his personal indignation.

Many of the Expressionists saw machines as ogres. Kafka himself had a neurotic fear of the telephone and was conscious that technology threatened to reduce man himself to a machine. In January 1913 he wrote to Felice that a dictaphone, or any machine, seemed to him a far more demanding and terrible taskmaster than any human; you could shout down a typist, send her away, you were her master, but a dictaphone ruled you, you were its slave, no better than a factory

Scene from *Metropolis* dir. Fritz Lang 1927

worker serving a machine (BrF. 241). Yet he showed a lively interest in technical progress, and was one of the first creative writers to describe the flight of the aeroplane, after visiting an air display at Brescia during one of his trips to Italy with Brod in 1909.

As in the two stories written in 1912, the absurdity of the situations in *America* can be seen in a humorous light by the reader who resists the narrative technique and disassociates himself from the viewpoint of the hero. Karl Rossmann as anxious participant in the scenes has little opportunity to register their comic potential, but even from what is essentially his report we can appreciate the broad farce of the massive Brunelda exerting such a powerful attraction on the tramps and undergoing a ritual of cleanliness in her sordid environment.

As the novel progresses it becomes more extravagant and stylized. The hotel which at first was of normal proportions turns into a concern of mythical magnitude. The apparently symbolic final chapter confirms this pattern of development away from realism. Many of the distortions of reality are presented in visual terms. The importance of the characters' physical appearance (many are enormous and almost all are larger than Karl), their gestures and expressions as keys to their thoughts and feelings, and the significance of the interiors correspond to Karl's reliance on outward impressions. This novel, and indeed

Scene from *The Cabinet of Dr Caligari* dir. Robert Wiene 1919

several of Kafka's works, may thus remind the reader of a Charlie Chaplin comedy, and the extravaganza of the final chapter may recall a Fellini film. Kafka was for a period from 1908 onwards a keen cinemagoer. The one-reel silent films of that era relied, like the Yiddish drama, on exaggerated expression and gesture, they exploited pictorial romanticism and were often tinted with colour to heighten emotional content. Akin to this last feature are the atmospheric interiors of Pollunder's country mansion or Brunelda's apartment. Karl's escape from pursuing policemen is reminiscent of the chase that was an inevitable part of early slap-stick films. Kafka's tendency to express psychological states in visual terms, which colours his diaries and letters as well as his stories, was almost certainly encouraged by his experience of the early cinema and of the Yiddish theatre. The strange occurrences he describes are similar to the distortions, transformations and disappearances of the trick films of the first decade of this century.

Each time Karl is judged by his superiors, he is to some extent guilty. Yet even if he is judged by his actions rather than by his intentions, which are almost beyond reproach, the verdicts and in particular their consequences are not proportionate to the crime. Karl believes in an abstract ideal of justice. His antagonistic attitude, which arises from his sympathy for the underdog or from his own involvement, does not allow him to achieve a clear or consistent formulation of this point, but essentially he demands judgement based on faith in

Scene from *Nosferatu* dir. Fritz Lang 1922

the character of the accused rather than on the letter of the law. In practice the person giving judgement does so from a position of involvement in the authoritarian system and is unwilling or unable to take account of the accused's intentions and of mitigating circumstances. In each case justice is equated with discipline. It is ironic that Karl, who believes in hard work and self-discipline, is the victim of an impersonal disciplinary system and of forces associated with licence. It is perhaps not fortuitous that he sees the Statue of Liberty as a figure holding a sword of justice (or vengeance) and not the torch of liberty.

Karl Rossmann, already rejected by his father, has a longing for friendship and protection, but no sooner are his emotions tied to one person than he yearns for another. Several of them operate as substitute father or mother figures. The father figure has been broadened to include any authority, a development which points forward to many of Kafka's later works.

With the exception of the fragmentary last chapter that defeats interpretation, the novel presents a comprehensible world, imperfect but ordered, which appears absurd or irrational to the person whose knowledge is severely limited. Karl Rossmann does not, like the heroes of Kafka's later novels, succumb to anxiety and bewilderment. *America* is more likely than *The Trial* or *The Castle* to satisfy the reader who looks for an entertaining story, yet it does not in such obvious measure as they evoke the feeling that the story has a multiplicity of possible

Scene from *Student of Prague* dir. Stella Rye 1913

relevances. The repetition of seduction and expulsion in the novel may, however, recall the Fall and suggest that the work has religious significance. Its partial derivation from the nineteenth-century novel distinguishes it from Kafka's two later novels. Yet it shares that technical advance which marked Kafka's solution to the problem of portraying the extraordinariness of life. In *Description of a Struggle* he had written as if completely bemused by experiences that did not make sense; in *Wedding Preparations* he had seized the ordinary; neither work has the power to convince the reader that reality has been apprehended in an unusual but significant manner. In the works written in 1912 and later the situations and events, however fantastic, seem to have their own inexorable logic and to reflect a fundamental truth. Surrealistic and realistic elements are combined.

There is some reason to suppose that in *America* Kafka was portraying somewhat ironically aspects of his own youthful attitude to the world. His vision of a different existence in a far off land is seen as an illusion. The way in which events are subsequently explained in the novel would seem to reflect the author's conviction, held when he was Karl Rossmann's age, that life was ultimately explicable. Yet there remains the dreamlike impression that arises from his disillusionment with schematic explanations of reality. That he portrayed in the novel an attitude to life which he had left behind or perhaps never really held is indicated in a letter to Felice where he wrote that only the first chapter derived from inner truth, and that he rejected almost all the rest of the work, since it had been written as if in recollection of a great but completely absent feeling (BRF. 332). He himself wept over one passage (BRF. 165), presumably over Karl Rossmann's invulnerability to guilt. In his last years he was moved by this youthful dream and saddened when a young friend inadvertently reminded him that he had lost his youth and the possibility of happiness associated with it. This friend, Gustav Janouch, recounts his conversation with Kafka about *The Stoker*:

'There is so much sunshine and high spirits in your story. So much love – though it is never mentioned.'

'They are not in the story, but in the subject of the story – youth,' said Franz Kafka gravely. 'Youth is full of sunshine and love. Youth is happy, because it has the ability to see beauty. When this ability is lost, wretched old age begins, decay, unhappiness.'

'So age excludes the possibility of happiness?'

'No, happiness excludes age.' Smiling he bent his head forward, as if to hide it between his hunched shoulders.

'Anyone who keeps the ability to see beauty never grows old.'

His smile, his attitude, his voice reminded one of a quiet and serene boy.

'Then in *The Stoker* you are very young and happy.'

I had hardly finished the sentence than his expression darkened.

'*The Stoker* is very good,' I hastened to add, but Franz Kafka's dark grey eyes were filled with grief.

'One speaks best about what is strange to one. One sees it most clearly. *The Stoker* is the memory of a dream, of something that perhaps never really existed. Karl Rossmann is not a Jew. We Jews are born old.' (J. 26)

This moving record, if true, points to the emotional involvement of Kafka in *America* and its early conception. Its hero is ignorant of despair or *Angst*, he has an 'innocence' that is not enjoyed by Kafka's later protagonists. For the author's relationship with Felice Bauer was to show that it was not possible, at least for him, to come to terms with reality. Karl Rossmann suffers humiliation but is not overcome by it; Kafka's feeling of humiliation at his constant failures to cope with life combined with a sense of insufficiency and guilt to become anguished self-recrimination.

Questions of guilt

The struggle to win Felice would perhaps continue for ever; certainly no fairy-tale princess had been fought for so relentlessly (BrF. 730): thus Kafka saw his relationship with Felice Bauer in October 1916, four years after it had begun and one year before it was finally ended. The forces taking part in the battle within his mind have already been mentioned: his ambivalent attitude towards marriage, his sense of unworthiness and his need for isolation. In January 1913 he wrote to her of his ideal of solitude, life in a cellar sealed off from the rest of the world (BrF. 250). Unlike Gregor Samsa in *The Metamorphosis*, he found impersonal hotel bedrooms comforting in contrast to the family apartment (BrF. 71). In 1911 he had expressed his view of the artist or writer who by his very nature must be isolated from other men; such a man, he wrote, must draw his strength exclusively from within himself (E. 317). This conviction remained unchanged after his meeting with Felice. Similarly his belief that no woman could feel love for him, only pity, dates back to at least 1907. In that year he had written to a girl whom he had met while on a visit to his uncle Siegfried, that if she liked him a little, then it was from pity, his part was fear (Br. 40). Yet he had repeated proof (which he found hard to credit) that Felice did love him, and he was fully conscious that he needed her in order to endure life. The choice between marriage (or 'life') and creative writing seemed a very real dilemma. When he made a choice, and decision did not come easily to him, he chose against marriage and in favour of writing, but since he did not want to reject 'life' altogether and could not dismiss his love for Felice the decision was inevitably further questioned and revoked. The choice of solitude was the easier one since it was a decision to continue the status quo. His uncertainty in all matters became, through the emotional and spiritual stress of his relationship with Felice, fear, fear of everything, most of all of the unknown.

The state of *Angst* which Kafka diagnosed in himself, fear of nothing in particular, but of everything in general, spiritual anguish, is according to Kierkegaard inevitably associated with guilt and reveals man's true relationship to the world and to himself. Kafka read Kierkegaard in August 1913 and found many of his own thoughts and feelings reflected in his philosophy: 'As I suspected, his case, despite essential differences, is very similar to mine, at least he is on the same side of the world. He bears me out like a friend' (T. 21.8.'13). In 1918 he corresponded with Brod on their reactions to Kierkegaard and stressed that certain religious ideas were common to Kierkegaard and Brod and implied that he shared them also. Kierkegaard, too, felt overwhelmed by his father, longed for marriage but could not wed, and suffered anguished loneliness. His rejection of logic and philosophical discussion, his protest on behalf of the suffering, his belief that no man can know his place or duty in the world, and his conviction that every action involved an anguished choice made in the dark are indeed paralleled in Kafka's life and works. Kierkegaard wrote from emotional involvement; a forerunner of Existentialism, his anti-intellectualism yet distinguishes him from Heidegger or Sartre. It is doubtful whether Kafka would have been so impressed by those more cerebral thinkers as he was by Kierkegaard.

The impossible choice to be made about Felice – he wrote in May 1913 that he could not live without her, nor with her (BRF. 380 f.) – became Kafka's almost sole preoccupation, for it concerned the whole pattern of his future life. Late in 1912 Brod had to intervene on his friend's behalf and assure Felice that Kafka loved her and explain his extreme sensitivity. But Brod had just become engaged and Kafka could not rely on his friendship for ever. From February 1913 until July 1914 he wrote no work of significance. Felice's failure to comment on *Meditation*, which had just appeared, worried him: did she not think of him as a writer? He became jealous when she praised books by others. In the absence of inspiration it was just as easy for him to assume that he might as well marry and give up an existence designed for writing as to conclude that his relationship with her deprived him of the opportunity or ability to write. He began to suffer more and more from headaches and took to various forms of physical exercise, walking, riding, rowing, swimming, and to part-time manual jobs in a carpenter's shop and as a gardener in an attempt to alleviate his mental condition and regain health. He could not now in honesty tell Felice that he was too busy writing to go and see her.

At Easter and Whitsun 1913 he went to Berlin, and on the second occasion was introduced to Felice's family. He now began to consider approaching her parents about an engagement, but still expressed strong doubts on this question in his letters to her, and in July 1913 drew up one of several inconclusive balance sheets showing the pros and cons of marriage in his particular case. In August he wrote to her father asking tentative approval for the match and received an encouraging reply, but not before he had composed another letter, which was never sent, but which would scarcely have produced such a favourable answer. For here he said that he lived for nothing but literature, lacked all aptitude for family life, found his job unbearable, and that Felice was bound to be unhappy with him (T. 21.8.'13). This letter employs on a smaller scale the technique of the later *Letter to My Father*: Kafka finds complications in apparently simple matters, places blame upon himself and yet by a façade of complete honesty absolves himself through confession. It seems that he desired above all an immutable decision and an end to doubt, preferably without taking the responsibility for the decision himself: he hoped, with part of his mind, that Felice or her family would decide against him, and with the other half, that she would accept him despite all the problems he insisted on describing to her in detail. Their engagement, still unofficial, was not irrevocable enough to thrust all doubts aside, and in September Kafka cancelled plans to spend a holiday with Felice and went to Vienna to attend a business conference and a Zionist meeting. The first break had taken place. It resulted from a deadening of his spirit under great stress:

> Imprisoned by inhibitions with which you are familiar, I am unable to move, I am utterly, but utterly incapable of suppressing the inner obstacles; the only thing I am still just capable of is to be immensely unhappy about it . . . and yet I think I feel this condition to be appropriate to myself, assigned to me by some superhuman justice, a condition . . . to be borne by me to the end of my days. . . . We shall have to part. (BRF. 466)

From Vienna Kafka travelled to Trieste, Venice and Verona and then spent a few weeks in a sanatorium in Riva, the resort on Lake Garda that he knew from his travels with Brod. There he met an eighteen-year-old Swiss girl, a certain G.W., with whom he was happy for a short time. He was still writing to Felice, declaring his love but rejecting marriage:

> Of the four men I consider to be my true blood relations (without comparing myself to them either in power or in range), of Grillparzer, Dostoyevsky, Kleist and Flaubert, Dostoyevsky was the only one to get married, and perhaps Kleist, when compelled by outer and inner necessity to shoot himself on the Wannsee, was the only one to find the right solution. (BrF. 460)

Kafka here names some of his spiritual cousins, tormented by self-doubt in their attitudes to love and marriage. Kleist and Flaubert were also close to him as writers: the German, an untypical Romantic, in his terse dramatic treatment of extraordinary events (Kafka was fond of reading his story of injustice, *Michael Kohlhaas*); the Frenchman in his dedication to stylistic perfection. Even more significant is the analogy with Dostoyevsky, who called himself a child of doubt and unbelief, knew the terrible torment caused by the desire to believe, who saw the evil rooted in man yet pitied him, was deeply moved by suffering, and plagued by the thought that none but God could understand and judge the minds and actions of men. Like Kafka he portrayed men torn by contradictory passions and compared them with animals – the hero of *Notes from the Underworld* says he would like to become an insect. The scope of his work is greater than Kafka's; his message of redemption through suffering and that life should be loved despite logic are not clearly echoed in Kafka. But both excel in the depiction of doubt and loneliness and of interiors that are prisons of the conscience. At this time Kafka was also reading Strindberg, whose despairing view of the relationship of the sexes must have increased his pessimism.

Felice now sent a friend to Prague to sound the situation. This friend, Grete Bloch, was a typist, four years younger than Felice and rather better-looking. Early in November Kafka went to Berlin but could see Felice for a few minutes only. On her suggestion they agreed to write to one another but not to think of marriage. This meeting was something of a humiliation for Kafka. Felice did not write at all frequently and he diagnosed that her love had cooled. He began to confide in Grete Bloch and built up a close relationship with her over the following year during which she mediated between him and Felice. Felice's resistance now acted as a spur to his love. His pride told him that he must make up for his previous failure by winning her. In

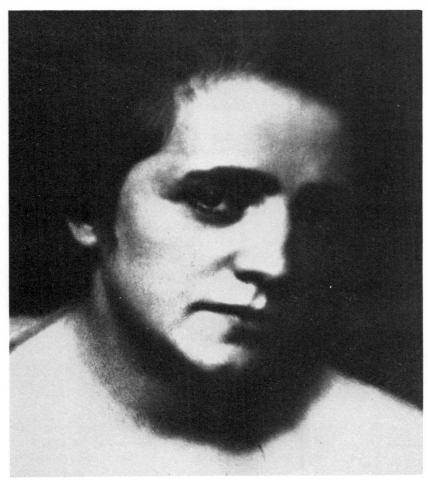

Grete Bloch

January 1914 he insisted that marriage was the only solution to their predicament and the only way of satisfying his need for her (BRF. 488). Evidently he had sensed that she was not interested in any other outcome. Felice simply acknowledged receipt of this letter, and Kafka had now to ask Grete Bloch to intercede on his behalf. Now Felix Weltsch became engaged and Kafka felt the need to marry even more strongly. At the end of February he went unannounced to Berlin.

Felice was friendly but would not commit herself. It is possible that she suspected an affair between Kafka and Grete Bloch, for he had to deny the extent of his correspondence with her friend. Yet at their next meeting, which would have been earlier had he had his way, at Easter 1914, Kafka and Felice Bauer were unofficially engaged once more. At the end of April the engagement was announced in the Berlin and Prague press. At the beginning of May Felice came to Prague to look for somewhere to live.

On 1 June there was a reception in Berlin, with both families present, to mark the official engagement. On 12 June it was ended. Kafka met Felice in an hotel in Berlin where in the presence of her father, her sister Erna, Grete Bloch and his friend Ernst Weiss, he was required to explain his attitude. Grete Bloch had, it seems, shown Felice passages from Kafka's letters written to her since the engagement which shed doubt on his desire to marry Felice. Probably Grete Bloch wished in this way to do the right thing by Felice because she felt guilty about her part in the affair. In the face of accusation Kafka scarcely defended himself. It is not clear whether he had planned to make Felice break off the engagement, or to end it himself, whether he welcomed or feared the confrontation, or whether he simply accepted its outcome. His feelings were certainly mixed. Before leaving for Berlin he wrote to his sister Ottla, promising her a letter in a day or two, but saying that for the moment he could not express what he felt, he knew only that there was a gulf between what he was thinking and what he ought to be thinking; he was utterly confused (BR. 130). The official engagement had been a shock to him, perhaps because Grete Bloch was present. His feelings for her had become more than mere friendship and his letters to her seem to suggest that he loved her rather than Felice. She had given him the strength to propose to Felice again; he could not afford to lose such a source of confidence. He insisted that their relationship must continue after the engagement, after the wedding, and hoped that her support would enable him to meet the problems of marriage.

When the engagement was broken off he maintained a façade of innocence but admitted his guilt to himself. He left Berlin for the Baltic coast, just as Austria delivered her ultimatum to Serbia. The international crisis overshadowed his personal predicament and he hurried back to his family. Within a few days of his return to Prague Europe was at war. He had to give up his dreams, entertained immediately after the break with Felice, of starting a new life, leaving his job, family and Prague and becoming an independent writer in Berlin or Munich.

Only very rarely did he comment on the war in his letters or diaries. He wrote of his hatred for the combatants, and called the patriotic parades in Prague 'the most disgusting accompaniments of the war' (T. 6.8.'14). Yet he was saddened by Austrian defeats. Not surprisingly, he did not, as a Jew, share the belief of many leading German writers at this time that the outbreak of war brought an end to class conflicts, a new sense of national unity and purpose, a new vitality and a new set of heroic values. He remained the sceptical outsider, and could not rejoice that much of what he longed for had apparently been found by others; rather he was, it seems, appalled by their self-deception. He was not called up for military service because of his job. His eldest sister and her family moved into the parental apartment when her husband was conscripted, and for the first time, at the age of thirty-one, Kafka rented a room of his own. He moved frequently in an attempt to find quieter quarters, being unable to tolerate the slightest noise. Again he was obliged to spend his afternoons in the factory belonging to his family. Obsessed with personal disappointments and moved by historic events, perhaps because of his immersion in the one and abhorrence of the other, he found a new determination to give his own existence its particular *raison d'être* and experienced in the following weeks a period of intense creation, similar to that of the autumn of 1912. To justify his failure with Felice he had to prove his worth as a writer. In the second half of 1914 he added a chapter to *America*, wrote most of *Der Prozess* (*The Trial*), one of his most gripping and most horrifying stories *In der Strafkolonie* (*In the Penal Settlement*), and another short narrative, *Der Riesenmaulwurf* (*The Giant Mole*). On 6 August he wrote in his diary: 'My talent for portraying my inner life has thrust all other matters into the background . . . Nothing else will ever satisfy me.'

The connections between *The Trial* and Kafka's relationship with Felice Bauer are general rather than specific. A girl with the same initials, Fräulein Bürstner, is somehow linked with the 'trial' of the hero and would probably have played a more important role had the work been finished. There may be a parallel between Fräulein Montag, Fräulein Bürstner's friend through whom she rejects the hero's advances, and Grete Bloch in her role as mediator. The women in the novel seem to be attracted to the hero in pity rather as Kafka suspected women felt

Manuscript page from *The Trial*

towards him. Kafka referred to the meeting in the Berlin hotel as a tribunal in which he was the accused, and called a letter he wrote the following day to Felice's parents a speech from the gallows (T. 23, 27.7.'14). Yet the novel is not about the hero's failure in his love for one woman and marriage does not enter his thoughts. Its main themes can be linked with preoccupations present in the author's mind as a general pattern into which the affair with Felice fitted as only one element, however important. *The Trial* and Kafka's other great novel *The Castle* have bewitched critics because in them, even more clearly than in his short stories, he transferred his personal problems and experiences on to a more general plane. In *The Trial* particularly there is a tendency to suggest interrelations between the most varied aspects of experience which at once fascinates and baffles the reader, and although it is incomplete it is one of the most impressive of his works. In crystal-clear language Kafka writes of most peculiar events and conversations, perplexing his reader and yet compelling him to read on in the hope of enlightenment. It is a very strange novel – so extraordinary, indeed, that few indisputable statements may be made about it. For the author does not allow the reader any certain knowledge about the world in which his hero lives, nor gives him any great insight into his thoughts.

Like Georg Bendemann, Joseph K. is suddenly made aware of an aspect of his own existence of which he was ignorant; like Gregor Samsa he awakes to find himself overcome by a strange and completely

Erich Heckel *The Lunatic* 1914

unexpected turn of fate. On Joseph K.'s thirtieth birthday he is informed that he stands accused of an unspecified crime and is to be tried by a court whose existence was unknown to him. One year later, at the end of the novel, he is executed: with little ceremony two servants of the court stab him on a piece of waste ground at the edge of the town where he lives. The 'arrest' at the beginning of the story does not prevent the hero from following his normal occupation in a bank and the whole trial is most unusual. Only a few facts are clear: Joseph K. is subjected to a trial or a process (the title of the novel allows both interpretations); the court is not part of the country's normal legal system; he is gradually exhausted mentally and reduced to frustration by the knowledge that he is accused and cannot defend himself; he becomes obsessed with his case to the exclusion of all else. At an age when traditionally a man settles down and achieves a firm basis for his existence, his life is disrupted. He never discovers what his guilt is or whether he is guilty. The novel is concerned less with specific guilt than with the effects on the hero's mind of the possibility, which is almost a certainty, that he is in some terrible but incomprehensible way guilty. It shows a world which is, if not the source, at least a mirror of his anxiety.

Joseph K. pays visits to a night-club dancer and neglects his family, but there is scarcely more than a hint that his failure to fit into a normal family life or to engage in responsible human relationships worries him or constitutes his supposed guilt. After his 'arrest' he lusts after Fräulein Bürstner whom he scarcely knows, is consumed with a brief passion for a married woman and is seduced by a maid, but he hardly sees these encounters as sinful. Since the story is related largely from the point of view of the hero the author gives little or no indication of the nature of his guilt. In a diary entry Kafka called Joseph K. guilty (T. 29.9.'15): but this may mean simply that he is found guilty by the mysterious court. His unwillingness to accept even the possibility of guilt may itself be his guilt and his downfall. The libidinous maid Leni advises him to admit his guilt as the only way to escape the court. He is told by the painter Titorelli, who is supposed to have contacts with court officials, that as far as is known the court never acquits an accused person totally: a case may be set aside temporarily, the accused provisionally or apparently acquitted, but he may be accused again later, presumably of the same crime; or judgement may be postponed indefinitely. Joseph K. sets his mind on a total acquittal which is outside known experience.

Joseph K. discovers little about the court. He learns that it is a vast organization, made up of judges, examining magistrates and officials of all kinds. He meets only its lowliest servants and one relatively inferior examining magistrate. Titorelli knows only gossip about the higher judges. Joseph K. engages a lawyer, Huld, who specializes in such cases, but his knowledge of the procedure of investigation and trial is very limited. The lawyer's position is unofficial, for the court does not recognize any form of defence. He does not even know the accusation levelled at his client. Joseph K. is told by the prison chaplain, whose position connects him with the court, that the court is attracted to the guilty person but that it will leave him alone unless he seeks contact with it; but the facts of the story do not entirely corroborate this. Perhaps he could have ignored the 'arrest', since he was free to live as before; and perhaps he could have ignored the summons to the first hearing, for it specified neither exact time nor place. After that first hearing it is his curiosity, or his anxiety, that attracts him to the court. Could he have established his innocence simply by ignoring the accusation, by rejecting it as ridiculous? Initially, indeed, he is tempted to do just that, but lacks the confidence to explore this possibility. Perhaps it is his guilty conscience that makes him so concerned about his own defence.

If this is so, then (we may continue to speculate) the court is right and the hero is guilty. Some servants and officials of the court are corrupt and many are probably inefficient. The two warders who arrest Joseph K. rob him of his breakfast and some of his clothes. The magistrate at the first hearing uses his authority to satisfy his sexual desires; his official files are full of pornographic scribblings. There is no evidence that petitions or statements submitted to the court are ever read. Yet the failings of the organization and its servants do not discredit the court as such. When the hero complains about the two warders, they are severely punished: the court has a code of discipline for its own members even if it is not always observed.

If the hero is guilty, his guilt may be existential and analogous to original sin. The court, we remember, is never convinced of the accused person's innocence. Joseph K. may stand for an average person who is suddenly confronted with the possibility or certainty of existential guilt, with the 'guilt', associated with *Angst*, that obsessed Kafka himself who saw the probability of guilt in all thought and action. Joseph K.'s ostensible refusal to admit guilt may perhaps be an arrogant and insensitive reaction to the problems of existence. Rather than admit its possibility he accuses the court of malpractice or argues that no man can be guilty since all are equal. This echo of an egalitarian attitude becomes nonsense since it admits its opposite: that all men may be guilty. It is, however, a comforting argument, as Kafka himself was aware. In the *Letter to My Father* he suggests that both he and his father might be absolved from blame since responsibility could be allocated to chance or fate or environment. Yet there Kafka continues to accuse his father, and Joseph K., just as he is about to concede possible guilt and to kill himself, decides to make his executioners take full responsibility and places the blame on the person, who might be God, who denied him the strength to commit suicide. In the novel the world seems to inspire guilt. Perhaps it is the fault of the Creator that this is so.

Joseph K. is not so sensitive or so prone to self-criticism as his creator. Yet while his conscious mind insists on his innocence he seems also to have doubts. For a supposedly innocent man he is very concerned about his public image. As time goes on he suspects, and is gradually convinced that his guilt is known to an increasing number of people; it is even possible that everyone he meets knows about his case. His reactions may be those of a man with a guilty conscience increasingly afraid that his secret might be public knowledge. The court itself might, indeed, be a reflection of his conscience. The dream-like atmosphere of the novel lends weight to an interpretation of this kind, according to which all the action takes place in the protagonist's mind. When Joseph K. looks into a junk room at the bank he finds there the two warders whom he had accused being whipped by the court whipper; days later he returns to the room and discovers the same scene still being enacted: this seems to mirror his continuing anxiety about the effect of his accusation. The location of the rooms in the house in which he boards changes: if this is not an oversight we may assume that the world around the hero is used to reflect his psychological state. Its darkness, oppressiveness and bewildering strangeness mirror his mental condition. Nevertheless this world and the other characters attain very real proportions.

It is possible that Joseph K. is the innocent victim of an unjust organization. The novel gives the impression that he could never prove his innocence and escape condemnation, yet it could be that a nagging and only half-admitted awareness of the possibility of guilt makes him fail to fight the court with the utter conviction necessary for success. Having made what is perhaps the initial mistake of heeding the court at all he is exhausted in an uneven battle. He is unable to take either of the courses which might lead to success: total inaction and refusal to accept the reality of the conflict or complete dedication to it. At decisive moments, in his interviews with the lawyer, Titorelli and the chaplain, at the first hearing and at the court offices, he allows himself to be distracted from his case or is physically or mentally unable to cope with the situation. Once existential guilt is sensed as a possibility the individual needs a faith or strength of will not possessed by Joseph K. to disprove or dismiss that possibility. Once a person with partial insight into his own inadequacy admits the existence of an authority competent to judge him his guilt is certain. These are two morals to be drawn from this line of interpretation of *The Trial*, which allows that the judging authority could be wrong, be it society, conscience, God, or any other person or system posited as accuser or judge.

Another possibility is that both hero and court are wrong. Then we have the paradox of the imperfect accusing and condemning the imperfect, a position which, however ludicrous when stated so baldly, is accepted as necessary in every social system. On his arrest one of the warders chides the hero for not accepting his situation. The lawyer tells him to come to terms with the position as it exists. The chaplain informs him that one need not consider everything to be true but must accept it as necessary. Joseph K. is perhaps looking (like Karl Rossmann) for an ideal in an imperfect world. Because this reading of the novel makes it a comment on a general human predicament which has been felt most acutely by recent generations, and because the hero's case seems to involve every aspect of his life, this is perhaps the most persuasive of the many possible interpretations of the work.

The portrayal of the court contains an element of social criticism. The endless hierarchy of officials, the procedural systems unfathomable to outsiders and even to members of the organization, the frustrating delays, and the impotence of the ordinary man in his dealings with bureaucracy reflect aspects of large organizations and state ministries in almost every society and notorious features of the Habsburg Empire. Even the situation of the court offices, in an ill-equipped and squalid attic of a tenement block, is not without parallel in reality. There may also be criticism of the hero's social attitudes. In his treatment of the court warders he wavers between arrogant superiority and sympathy. His uneasiness towards three lowly bank employees who are inexplicably present at his arrest seems to arise from a fear that his position of respect and authority is open to question. Yet if the novel is simply a critical comment on social problems and a reflection of the author's ambivalent attitude towards, for example, socialism and bureaucracy (he was a disillusioned critic of institutional bureaucracy with a reluctant admiration for its self-sufficiency and permanence), Kafka seems to have overplayed the complexity of this subject-matter.

Joseph K. seeks help and enlightenment from women, from a lawyer, a painter and a priest. In the women he looks for sensual pleasure, but also for practical help through their tenuous connections with the law or the court. He hopes for sympathy, advice and companionship, someone to distract him from his problem or to help him shoulder it. There may be a hint that the women are important to him because of their supposed influence on public opinion or their ability to make the individual ignore it. Of the lawyer, the artist and the priest, the first is the least help to the hero, who eventually decides to dispense with his services. His action may reflect Kafka's disillusionment with the law as a means to justice and a source of truth. The amazement with which Huld and others greet Joseph K.'s decision to dismiss him makes more sense if the relationship between client and lawyer is seen as one between a person with a guilty secret in need of help and someone in whom he confides and is therefore obliged to treat with circumspection. The artist Titorelli is somewhat more helpful, but like Huld he is a dubious and grotesque character. Admittedly he is not presented as a genius, but his personality and the restrictedness of his subject matter could mirror the author's doubts about art or literature as a means to enlightenment. The assured superiority of the priest may reflect Kafka's belief that religion held the answers to the problems of existence even if faith were denied him and his hero. Ultimately, as Joseph K. is told by the priest, and as he begins vaguely to realize, no second person can help him, he must rely on himself. His is a personal problem, although not without parallels (there are other accused men), and its implications seem to bridge many spheres of experience, psychological, social, philosophical and religious.

Kafka's diffidence towards his father developed into, or was paralleled by, an inordinate sense of insecurity, fear and guilt in his relations with other people and the world in general. In the *Letter to My Father* he referred to Joseph K.'s feelings before his execution in order to illustrate his own: 'I had lost my self-confidence where you were concerned, and in its place had developed a boundless sense of guilt. (In recollection of this boundlessness I once wrote of someone, accurately: "He is afraid that the shame will outlive him.")' (H. 196).

Other people and life in general seemed to make unquestionable, but often unacceptable or unjust claims upon him. The court of the novel has many characteristics of Kafka's father figure. It is imperfect yet has absolute authority, it is half accepted and half rejected by the hero.

If *The Trial* represents a world experienced by a man divided in himself, unsure of his standing in reality, then it is logical for it to include a religious aspect. The parable of the doorkeeper has undoubted relevance to the hero's predicament. A 'man from the country' seeks admittance to the 'Law' but is denied access by the doorkeeper. From him the man learns that even if he were allowed through this first door there are many others to pass, guarded by more powerful doorkeepers. The doorkeeper accepts bribes but is not moved and offers the man no hope; yet the man waits. After many years he dies, as the keeper closes the door, saying that this entrance was intended for him, and a glimpse of the light radiating from the 'Law' is caught shining from the far interior of the building. The story seems to say that entry is impossible, that there is a way, particular to the individual, but that it is barred. The 'Law' sheds light; its name implies a codified system ruling human existence and deciding on guilt and innocence. It is perhaps the law of existence in all its facets; it may well be similar in function to the Law of Judaism. Is there then a system and meaning governing life which is yet beyond the reach of the individual? As the ensuing conversation between the priest and the hero shows, the story is open to most contradictory interpretations. The only apparently satisfactory attitude to adopt towards it is one of acceptance of what is seemingly absurd. This attitude Joseph K. cannot adopt.

Kafka hoped to find a meaning in life and to express it in his writings. What he found was a set of paradoxes. He suffered from feelings of guilt yet liked to argue his innocence. He was both attracted to and repelled by those figures and things that instilled this feeling of guilt in him. He wanted to be accepted by his father, to prove his normality, yet wished to retain and enhance his 'abnormal' individuality. He was not sure whether the reality he observed was true reality or distorted by his own vision. There are clear parallels between this, the author's reactions to life, and Joseph K.'s reactions to his trial. The hero's anxieties reflect the insecurity of a Jew in a hostile land.

The Trial refuses to yield the secrets of its paradoxes. Although much becomes meaningful when the hero's predicament is compared with Kafka's, Joseph K. is not identical with the author. Yet writing the novel helped Kafka to a better understanding of his own situation

(T. 15.10.'14), and seven years later, when staying in a hotel, he made, with amusement and apprehension, the following diary entry: 'Despite my having legibly written down my name, despite their having correctly written to me twice already, they have Joseph K. down in the directory. Shall I enlighten them, or shall I let them enlighten me?' (T. 27.1.'22). The novel has many messages, complementary and perhaps even contradictory. Despite its ambiguity and its incompleteness it has a unity and a sense of direction and purpose. On a larger scale than *The Judgement* and *The Metamorphosis*, and with even greater impact, it presents a world that is absurd yet horribly real. This world bears little resemblance to ordinary experience, but is made up of the elements of normal life. *The Trial* is deeply disquieting.

Of all Kafka's works *In the Penal Settlement* perhaps best merits the title of a horror story. Published in 1919, this gruesome tale was written in October 1914 during a pause in the composition of *The Trial*, and like that novel is concerned with justice in the form of punishment. In *The Trial* the hero is told at the time of his arrest that as his case progresses he will come to feel his guilt: this metaphor becomes reality in this story. An explorer visiting a penal settlement is shown an execution machine. The accused is strapped face downwards on to the machine and in the course of twelve hours an arrangement of ever more deeply cutting edges inscribes on his back the law that he has broken. According to the officer in charge the accused gains insight into his guilt and his face shines with knowledge as he dies. The officer says that a trial is not necessary: any defence would simply obscure the issue and waste time since guilt is beyond all doubt. Even more clearly than in *The Trial*, this judicial system does not admit the possibility of innocence.

The officer believes fanatically in the machine and its method of justice; he almost worships its inventor, the former commandant of the colony. The new commandant has not encouraged the preservation and maintenance of the machine. He is more interested in building a harbour and, according to the officer, is unduly influenced by women. The old commandant is referred to as if he were a god – he could apparently do everything – and some inhabitants of the colony believe that he will rise from the dead. It is not difficult to associate the old commandant with the God of the Old Testament; the process of execution as a means to recognition of guilt is similar to the autos-da-fé of the Inquisition: in the good old days, says the officer, crowds came to enjoy the edifying spectacle. The new commandant with his economic and possibly more humanitarian bias seems to present a more modern outlook.

The explorer sees a prisoner placed on the apparatus, fearful but unaware of what is to happen. He has failed to comply with an apparently senseless order and the sentence 'Obey thy superior' is to be inscribed into his flesh before he is torn to pieces. The new commandant's women friends have succeeded in giving him sweets with the result that he vomits over the machine, much to the annoyance of the officer. This prisoner does not die. Distressed that the visitor is not convinced of the rightness of the procedure, the officer, almost alone in his belief in it and apprehensive lest the explorer should persuade the new commandant to abolish it, decides to prove his faith in the system. He removes the prisoner from the machine, adjusts it with much effort and explains that it is now ready to inscribe the sentence 'Be just'. He then straps himself into it. The apparatus functions unpredictably, smashes the body of the officer and disintegrates. The explorer is appalled.

He runs away and does not pause to consider the implications of the officer's death. It is left to the reader to do this – though he, too, may not be in a mood for rational analysis. Possibly the machine had not been adequately maintained, in which case nothing can be deduced about the guilt or innocence of the officer or the validity of the system. The officer seems in any case to have made a logical error – or rather his action is irrational: if he is innocent, if he had always been just, the machine would be at a loss since it is designed to deal with guilt; if he is guilty of previous injustice and were to experience transfiguration this would presumably indicate that the system was not perfect since it had been misused in the past. Moreover the officer is not ignorant of the sentence to be inscribed into his flesh and cannot expect enlightenment.

Kafka felt that life itself was a process of punishment beyond normal concepts of justice. There was in his mind a connection between the atmosphere of the story and the world in which he lived. When his publisher criticized the horror of the tale he wrote to him that it was not alone in being distressing, for they lived in an age of torture, and his own afflictions were greater than those of the age in general (BR. 150). In the story the process of punishment is observed by an outsider, not by a sufferer as in *The Trial*. The gruesome details are related in a matter-of-fact style, and there is no hysterical sensationalism. Nevertheless the question of the sense or senselessness of the action remains unanswered, and this uncertainty increases the horror. The ending is intentionally inconclusive. It seems to imply that the system of torture can never be completely destroyed and that any attempt to alleviate the suffering it causes does not improve matters. The story reflects Kafka's frustrated desire for certainty, even if it was the certainty that life was torture, provided that this torture had a meaning.

The Trial and *In the Penal Settlement* develop the theme of punishment found in *The Judgement*, but the punishing authority is now a system or organization and there is a more pronounced tendency to question the validity of its procedures. Kafka had become even more critical of the demands imposed upon him from without, but this apparent increase in self-confidence involved a still greater awareness of the possibility of guilt: guilt brought by the very act of refusing to accept what was ordained.

Ein Traum (*A Dream*) might well have been included in *The Trial*, though it was published as part of the later collection of stories, *A Country Doctor*. In this short sketch Joseph K. dreams that he walks into a graveyard. He stops by a fresh mound of earth. A gravestone has just been erected beside it, and an artist begins to write an inscription. Seeing Joseph K., he hesitates in embarrassment when he comes to the name and stops after a large letter J. Joseph K. realizes what is happening, scoops away the earth from the grave, which is apparently empty, slips into the hole and, with a feeling of rapture, watches the artist complete the inscription. At this moment he wakes. Kafka offers no comment.

In *The Trial* Joseph K. is not inclined to put his faith in a second person. Another accused man, the businessman Block who lives only for his case and depends entirely on the lawyer Huld, fills the hero with disgust and is, indeed, reduced to servitude. The individual in need of help confides his need to another and is then for ever bound to that person. In an unfinished story written in December 1914, *The Giant Mole*, Kafka explores a frustrating and ludicrous relationship between two men, one of whom wishes to help the other in an apparently hopeless situation. The younger man's embarrassment has been seen by some to reflect Kafka's attitude towards eastern Jewry, or the emotions of an agnostic who admires religious conviction in another. Significantly the tale ends as the young man feels that he will never be able to withdraw from his commitment to the other, despite his wish to do so. The story also seems to comment on the impossibility of writing convincingly about an aspect of life which no one will recognize or take seriously, except a previous writer who has been unsuccessful himself. For by the end of 1914 Kafka was once more despairing of his creative ability.

A soldier and his wound

In October 1914 the relationship between Kafka and Felice Bauer entered a new stage. Its resumption may be explained partly by Kafka's indecisiveness and partly by the attraction he had for Felice. Other women, too, were drawn to his good looks and responded intuitively to his need for help and understanding. He in turn was attracted to women who offered him sympathy. Since August he had been corresponding with Felice's sister Erna, who had felt sorry for him after the 'tribunal' in Berlin. His male acquaintances, too, found him likeable, though strange. For in company he invariably gave an impression of quiet content, quite different from what one would expect from reading his own self-analysis. Furthermore he was generally considerate, tactful, generous and reliable.

Grete Bloch, who was herself drawn to Kafka, wrote to him suggesting that a rapprochement with Felice was possible and desirable. She presumably felt partly responsible for the breakdown of the engagement and for Felice's subsequent distress. Now his readiness to repair the hurt done to Felice balanced his determination to maintain his independence. He began to write to Felice again, but less often, at less length, and less passionately than before. He had learnt that they could not achieve complete understanding through correspondence, and, besides, their letters were subject to the wartime censorship. Often he wrote postcards since these passed the censor more quickly. He doubted whether Felice could ever understand his dedication to writing and attributed the failure of their relationship to her refusal or inability to accept it as an essential part of his character. He saw her desire for a normal, stable, middle-class home as a barrier to their union. He still kept to his routine of working at night and was relatively content. But he could never be really happy, he thought, because there were two persons inside him, one of whom still longed for Felice and marriage. This half of him was wooed by Felice over the next two years, but until July 1916 he saw little hope of any change. Doubtless he was depressed by the war. His family and office work were repugnant to him as always; the latter must have seemed all the more senseless in the war situation. His writing was now so important to him that he scarcely hesitated to compare his search for quiet in which to write with the efforts of the combatants: 'Don't laugh, Felice, don't look upon my suffering as despicable; no doubt many people are suffering nowadays, and the cause of their suffering is something more than whispers in the next room; at best, however, they are fighting for their existence, or rather for the bonds connecting their existence to that of the community, and so do I, and so does everyone' (BRF. 627 f.).

In January 1915 Kafka and Felice met for a few hours in Bodenbach, the last stop within Bohemia on the Prague–Berlin railway. He seems to have agreed to the meeting reluctantly, and judged that it achieved nothing since neither of them had changed. Yet there was still, he felt, some sense in continuing to seek to improve their relationship. Over the next fifteen months he complained frequently of headaches and insomnia, and notes of deep depression are found in his diary: '3 May (1915). Completely indifferent and apathetic . . . Nothing, nothing. Emptiness . . . meaninglessness, weakness.' '21 Nov (1915). Complete futility'. It was an unproductive period. His records of a visit to Vienna with his sister Elli in April 1915, and of his study in October of that year of Napoleon's Russian campaign seem to reflect a need to fill his mental vacuum with factual reality, past or present. The publication of *The Metamorphosis* and the receipt of a literary prize for *The Stoker* late in 1915 gave him at best temporary consolation. The *Fontanepreis* had originally been awarded to the successful dramatist Carl Sternheim, who, needing neither publicity nor money, handed the prize on to Kafka.

From 1915 until the end of the war Kafka was involved in organizing the reception and rehabilitation of soldiers sent home from the front; he was particularly concerned with those who were suffering from nervous complaints. As a result of this work he was recommended for an official award, but the recommendation, although favourably received, was overtaken by the end of hostilities and of Austrian rule in Bohemia. In the winter of 1915–16 he tried unsuccessfully to have his exemption from military service cancelled. He dreamt of release from the office, his family and Prague, and was probably longing for death as well as greater involvement in the community struggle.

A turning-point came in July 1916 when Kafka and Felice spent ten days together in Marienbad. They decided to marry once the war was over and to live in Berlin: she would continue her work and he would be free to write. Kafka must have believed that she had realized that his writing came before everything else and that there was a possibility that she would not interfere with it. In any case in a period of literary sterility he could not justify his stand against marriage. He wrote to Brod from Marienbad: 'I found my way a little, she who had always extended a helping hand into the utter emptiness helped once more, and I entered into a relationship with her of human being to human being such as was unknown to me before. . . . But now I saw the look of trust in a woman's face and could not shut myself off against it. . . . I have no right to fight against it' (BR. 139).

His health improved somewhat, or at least he felt better despite headaches and insomnia. But the conflict in his mind was by no means resolved. He had simply, as he wrote in his diary, allowed himself to be drawn towards a future he feared because he recognized that he could not foresee or determine the future: 'One cannot spare oneself, one cannot calculate things in advance. You have not the slightest idea of what would be better for you' (T. 27.8.'16). Instead of exulting that he had once more come closer to the goal of marriage he attributed his 'success' to his weakness. Often he could look on examples of his own passivity with humour. Once, as a worthy *Herr Doktor* in his thirties, he meekly allowed himself to be mistaken for a lad who would willingly earn a few coppers by taking a gentleman for a trip in a rowing boat (BRM. 188). But the present situation was more serious, for it meant abandoning his vision of himself as the solitary genius, and he concluded that he must discard as a folly his habit of comparing himself with the great lonely writers and thinkers of the past: 'Never again debase yourself so that you become the battlefield of a struggle fought without regard for you and of which you feel only the terrible blows of the combatants. Rise up then. Mend your ways, escape officialdom, begin to see yourself as you are instead of calculating what you should become. Your first task is clear: become a soldier. Give up also those nonsensical comparisons you like to make between yourself and a Flaubert, a Kierkegaard, a Grillparzer. That is simply infantile – Flaubert and

Prague, the Charles IV Bridge

Kierkegaard knew very well how they stood, were men of decision, did not calculate but acted . . .' (T. 27.8.'16).

He did change a little in the following months, if only because he had wearied of trying to analyse and resolve his own problems. General observations and fragments of stories, written in his notebooks in the winter of 1916–17, replaced personal diary entries. He was trying to become less introvert. At one remove he became involved in work which satisfied his social conscience and his desire to identify with the Jews. He persuaded Felice to become a volunteer part-time teacher of Jewish refugee children in Berlin. Interested in progressive educational reforms, he was able to advise her on pedagogic aids and methods. His correspondence thus became more practical. Perhaps, however, he hoped that through her contact with the poor Felice might lose some of her bourgeois attitudes and become a more amenable marriage partner. In Prague he helped Brod in his efforts to assist Jewish refugees from Galicia. Brod put heart and soul into everything he did: writing novels and plays, critical and philosophical essays, Zionist propaganda, proclaiming unrecognized genius (he discovered Janaček). A provocative man, he often relied on Kafka's greater sensitivity in matters of tact.

Almost as soon as marriage loomed as a possibility once again, the writer in Kafka, who rejected marriage, arose from his sleep: he who had been benumbed by senseless routine began to struggle with the problems of creative writing (this is almost certainly what Kafka meant when he determined to become a 'soldier'). He produced a number of short stories, many of which were, however, left incomplete. Since the Marienbad meeting he had used a tiny house belonging to his sister Ottla situated below the Hradčany Palace in Prague. He rejoiced at being able to lock the door to the street. In November 1916, contrary to his usual practice, he took part in a public reading in Munich, where he read *In the Penal Settlement* and some pieces by Brod, who was unable to appear in person. Felice travelled from Berlin to be there, and Kafka returned to Prague rather encouraged. In March 1917 he rented a flat in an eighteenth-century aristocratic town house, the Schönborn Palais, also below the Hradčany hill. He and Felice planned to live here for a few months when they were married as soon as the war had ended.

Some of the stories written between September 1916 and June 1917, in his sister's house in the Alchimistengasse and in the Schönborn Palais, were prepared for publication in 1917. After some delay they appeared under the title *Ein Landarzt* (*A Country Doctor*). None of them is obviously connected with Felice Bauer, and many are among the most difficult of his works to interpret, though crystal clear on the surface. They vary from a few lines to several pages in length; some are related in content but there is no one clear, unifying theme. Signs of a happier outlook on life are few, but the first and last piece (and Kafka was concerned about their order) have a note of renunciation and whimsy.

The opening piece, *Der neue Advokat* (*The New Attorney*), reflects on the situation of the lawyer Dr Bucephalus who was once the battle horse of Alexander the Great. Times too have changed beyond recognition. Before, the king could lead his men towards the ultimate goal of India even if it were beyond human reach. Now the goal is even more distant and still more unattainable, and wars and leaders do not give a sense of purpose and direction, they simply confuse. Bucephalus has perhaps therefore, in today's social situation', chosen the best course in preferring contemplation and study to action. There are hints of a connection with Kafka and Prague: 'For many Macedonia is too confining, so that they curse Philip, the father . . .' The story seems to offer tentative justification not only for Kafka's eschewal of action but also for his reader, who, like Bucephalus, chooses to turn the pages of books far from the noise of battle. Above all it may be read as a comment on an existence, and an age, lacking in purpose.

The final story of the collection, *Ein Bericht für eine Akademie* (*A Report to an Academy*), describes a different reaction to a related existential situation. Its mood is part comic, part sad, with an undertone of despair. An ape reports how he has become almost human. Caught in Africa by a circus company, he lost his original freedom for ever;

indeed he cannot now remember what freedom was. Once in a cage aboard ship he could see no possibility of a return to freedom, so he aimed for something less. By 'aping' mankind he has reached, as he reports with ironic and sad satisfaction, the standard of the average European, and is a popular performer on the variety stage. Again the ape can in some ways be compared with Kafka. Almost five years separate him from apedom, says the ape; almost five years had passed since Kafka had met Felice when he wrote this story. Kafka knew that any success he had had, or would achieve, in becoming a normal member of society was a result of acting and denying his real self. The ape declares firmly that he is only making a report, not appealing for anyone's verdict.

One of Kafka's deepest desires, which he had expressed in his portrayal of Karl Rossmann, was to be accepted and not to be judged. He rejected even positive appraisals of his achievements in life and literature, and not just from modesty. The ape's report may also express Kafka's predicament as a writer. Five years had elapsed since he had experienced the liberation of writing *The Judgement*. Perhaps now he felt that he could only report on an art lacking in true inspiration, on a deliberate and desperate attempt at self-preservation and self-expression which was only partially successful. For could his strange visions be presented in normal language without becoming as untrue to themselves as a performing monkey?

In the story which gives its title to the collection, the country doctor is mysteriously given the opportunity to achieve the impossible, but only to meet another insoluble problem. One winter's night he is called out to a neighbouring village, but he has no horse and no one will lend him one. Two horses emerge miraculously from an empty pigsty and take him to his patient. Yet he is forced to abandon his maid to the attentions of a bestial groom who appears from nowhere with the horses. In fulfilling his duty, and satisfying his desire to help the patient, the doctor has to do violence to another emotion, his concern for the maid. This appears to be a comment on the divided self and the impossibility of complete moral self-satisfaction. The doctor finds nothing wrong with the patient, a young boy. But a second examination reveals an open sore, symbolizing a spiritual wound, but described in physical terms with nauseating vividness. No one can help the boy, for the community has ceased to believe in the ability of the priest. The doctor might just as well have stayed at home; he can only diagnose the boy's condition, which is apparently the result of extreme innate sensitivity: the doctor says that many are exposed to the instrument that caused the wound, but few are actually touched by it. He flees from the inopportune demands of patient and family and rides away naked into a snowstorm: 'Never shall I reach home. . . . Naked, exposed to the frost of this most unhappy of ages, with an earthly vehicle, unearthly horses, old man that I am, I wander astray. . . . Betrayed! Betrayed! A false alarm on the night bell once answered – it cannot be made good, not ever.' This is one of the rare places where Kafka interprets one of his own symbols – the winter stands for spiritual desolation associated with the modern age. The story abounds in possible allusions. It concerns a man swept off by primordial forces into a hell of frustration from which there is no escape. The unearthly horses may represent the power of inspiration that promised Kafka fulfilment but carried him away to a devastating reminder of his helplessness. The colour (*rosa*, pink) of the patient's wound, that symbol of lack of fitness for life, recalls the name of the maid, Rosa, through whom the doctor first becomes aware of his own vulnerability.

Some of the stories in this collection are almost certainly comments on other stories written or read by Kafka;* in two of them, *Elf Söhne* (*Eleven Sons*) and *Die Sorge des Hausvaters* (*The Cares of the Family Man*), he talks of his own works as if they were his sons and questions the value of this substitute family; whether they were intended to have a more general meaning is not certain. Yet even when such a piece defies interpretation, it impresses through its style: each word, phrase, sentence and paragraph has been carefully weighed. Kafka's mastery of prose rhythm is all the more effective in his short prose poems. One of these, *Auf der Galerie* (*Up in the Gallery*), consists of two short paragraphs, each one long sentence. Both portray a girl performer riding bareback in a circus. In the first paragraph the act and the audience's response is mechanical, repetitive, senseless and cruel. In the second paragraph the rider shows great skill and daring, she and the audience enjoy themselves. The first picture is presented as an imaginary one: if it were like that, writes Kafka, perhaps a young man in the gallery would run down to the ring and call for it all to stop. But since it is as described in the second paragraph, the man weeps. The two pictures describe the same thing, but in a different light. Which is the true picture? Does the circus represent the world? These questions remain unanswered, indeed they are not even formulated by Kafka. Nor does

* Cf. M. Pasley, 'Drei literarische Mystifikationen Kafkas' in J. Born etc., *Kafka – Symposion*.

Erich Heckel *White Circus Horses* 1921

he tell us whether the man weeps because the spectacle is so beautiful, or because it is senselesss, or because it is both at once. The man himself can scarcely know, for he is not even aware of his own tears.

Perhaps the best known of the stories from *A Country Doctor*, apart from the legend of the doorkeeper *Vor dem Gesetz (Before the Law)*, here removed from its context in *The Trial*, is another parable of exclusion, *Eine kaiserliche Botschaft (An Imperial Message)*. The emperor's message can never arrive, the distance is too great, the obstacles are too many, and even if it did the emperor would be dead. 'Yet you sit at your window when evening falls and dream it to yourself.' The message must be very important, yet its content is unknown. It may not even exist at all. The story is a poignant comment on Kafka's longing for certainty about the meaning of life.

An Imperial Message is taken from a longer narrative which Kafka did not publish, *Beim Bau der chinesischen Mauer (The Great Wall of China)*, where it functions as an example of the gulf of space and ignorance which separates the ordinary citizen from the emperor in Peking. The narrator wonders why the Great Wall was built in piecemeal fashion. It can only be, he thinks, because to complete a small section, unconnected with similar sections elsewhere, gave the people a sense of short-term satisfaction. The isolated segments of the wall, like fragments of knowledge, are sources of satisfaction in themselves, but useless unless connected to a greater whole. It is said that the wall, if completed, might serve as the foundations for a new Tower of Babel. Does this mean that once earthly life is secured man could ascend to heaven? The narrator does not understand it all, he concludes simply that no normal man will ever know the real purpose of the wall.

On the Laurenziberg in Prague, only a few steps from the Schönborn Palais, stood sections of a wall which had been erected simply to occupy convicts. In Kafka's hands this construction became a compelling symbol for man's drive to fortify the boundaries of his spiritual existence, and the starting-point for a series of disturbing questions.

The narrator of *The Great Wall of China* observes that ignorance does not worry many citizens; they are quite content in their belief that emperors long since dead are still alive, and happy to observe laws which belong to the past. It would not be far from the truth to say that they have no emperor, yet they are devoted to their emperor, who is largely if not wholly a fiction. The possible implications of this situation are manifold. Kafka could have been thinking of those who professed allegiance to a body politic, the Habsburg Empire or the pan-German Reich, whose reality was questionable. Equally well he could have been commenting on the function of outdated philosophies or religious beliefs.

A few themes and images occur repeatedly in these stories: horror and panic at isolation and exposure to danger; men and beasts lusting after warm blood; exposure to deadly cold; imprisonment. Yet there is also an attempt to understand the attitudes of those who do not feel such exposure or imprisonment, or who at least find a way, however dubious, of coming to terms with their predicament. Kafka knew that to ask certain questions about life was dangerous, even fatal. This insight seems to be expressed in a sketch written at this time, in the winter of 1916–17, called *Die Brücke* (*The Bridge*). The bridge is a man, poised over a chasm. But why is he there, he asks? For as a bridge he is useless unless someone passes over him, and this is unlikely, for he is far from habitation, roads or paths. Then one day he hears someone approaching and preparing to cross the bridge. The man who is the bridge faces downwards, but he must know who it is who steps on to his back, he turns over, collapses and falls to his doom.

Eruptions of irrational, threatening or destructive powers are found throughout Kafka's work. Yet they form a particularly frequent theme in these stories and fragments written during the war. It may be that Kafka's personal sense of exposure to such threats was strengthened by the thought that others were involved in a fight with forces that menaced civilized and rational human values.

A Country Doctor, in its hallucinatory vision and direct emotional impact, recalls *The Judgement*, *The Metamorphosis* and *In the Penal Settlement*. *The Great Wall of China* and *A Report to an Academy* are also grotesque, but less dramatic, and their more reflective and discursive manner appeals primarily, but not exclusively, to the intellect. Several of the stories written in the winter of 1916–17 fall somewhere between these two types, the one based on an obsessive image that seems to have overwhelmed the author with its immediacy, the other on a symbol that appears more consciously developed into action and description. The tireless probing of a problem in its many aspects and implications, often associated with the second type, is not unlike rabbinical commentaries on Jewish sacred writings. Compared with Kafka's earlier works these stories composed in the middle of the war show a greater interest in the possibility of remaining ignorant of absurdity or of avoiding its full destructive impact. Yet just as the writer was still involved in that particular trial which was his relationship with Felice, so his work was overshadowed by the moods of helplessness and destruction which had characterized *The Trial*. That novel also contained the reactions to absurdity and horror which are found again, in further variations, in these later narratives.

The second official engagement between Kafka and Felice Bauer took place early in July 1917. She came to Prague, and he suffered the formalities with a heavy heart. He sent the manuscript of the *Country Doctor* collection to his publisher and then the couple left for Hungary to visit Felice's sister.

The engagement of 1914 had lasted a month. This one was similarly short-lived. Shortly after Felice had returned to Berlin, and he to Prague, early in August 1917, he coughed blood. Four weeks later he reported the situation to Felice, who had suspected that something was amiss: 'Two days after my last letter, precisely four weeks ago, at about 5 a.m., I had a haemorrhage of the lung. Fairly severe; for ten minutes or more it gushed out of my throat; I thought it would never stop. The next day I went to see a doctor, who on this and several subsequent occasions examined and x-rayed me; and then, at Max's

Kafka with Felice Bauer; photograph taken when they became engaged for the second time in the summer of 1917

insistence, I went to see a specialist. Without going into all the medical details, the outcome is that I have tuberculosis in both lungs. That I should suddenly develop some disease did not surprise me; nor did the sight of blood; for years my insomnia and headaches have invited a serious illness, and ultimately my maltreated blood had to burst forth; but that it should be . . . tuberculosis . . . does surprise me' (BrF. 753). He seems to have believed the worst at once, for it confirmed his vision of himself as the cursed genius; the specialist first diagnosed catarrh in the lungs with a danger of T.B.

Kafka had spent several short periods in sanatoria, but these were centres of nature-healing and his visits more or less holidays. To go to a conventional T.B. sanatorium was a different matter, and he resisted such a step. He believed that normal medicine ignored the interconnection of body and mind and was convinced that his illness had spiritual causes. Perhaps even before his condition was diagnosed (the notebook entry is dated August or September 1914), he wrote that, in case he were soon to die or become a complete invalid, 'let me say that I myself have torn myself to shreds. . . . The world – F. is its representative – and my ego are tearing my body apart in a conflict that there is no resolving' (H. 131 f.). In September he commented in his diary that it was the age of his wound (by which he meant his illness), and not its physical characteristics, that made it painful. He wrote to Brod that he had himself predicted his illness when describing the bleeding wound in *The Country Doctor* (BR. 160). A few years later he was to refer to his *Angst* as a wound (BRM. 214) and to give his own

Edvard Munch
Fear 1896
(detail)

diagnosis its most vivid formulation: 'What happened was that the brain could no longer endure the burden of worry and suffering heaped on it. It said, "I give up; but should there be someone still interested in the maintenance of the whole, then he must relieve me of some of my burden and things will still go on for a while." Then the lung spoke up, though it probably didn't have much to lose anyhow. These discussions between brain and lung which went on without my knowledge may have been terrible' (BRM. 13). To Felice he wrote in September 1917: 'As you know, there are two combatants at war within me. . . . By word and silence, and a combination of both, you have been kept informed of the progress of the war for five years. . . . For secretly I don't believe this illness to be tuberculosis, at least not primarily tuberculosis, but rather a sign of my general bankruptcy. . . . The blood issues not from the lung, but from a decisive stab delivered by one of the combatants. . . . I am going to tell you a secret which at the moment I don't even believe myself (although the distant darkness that falls about me at each attempt to work, or think, might possibly convince me), but which is bound to be true: I will never be well again. Simply because it is not the kind of tuberculosis that can be laid in a deck-chair and nursed back to health, but a weapon that continues to be of supreme necessity as long as I remain alive' (BRF. 755 f.).

The only hope was to find a refuge from mental strain. This meant giving up his job, leaving his family, and breaking with Felice.

Over the past year or so he had come closer to his youngest sister Ottla, who, like him, had proved a wayward child in the eyes of their father. Despite her father's opposition she had started to run a farm in a remote Bohemian village. This was a bid for independence and a return to 'nature' which met her brother's full approval. Kafka now went to live with her in Zürau (Siřem): an escape from Prague and from his parents. He was granted convalescent leave from the office for the next eight months.

To break with Felice was more painful, and yet Kafka considered it inevitable: he believed that he had been proved unfit for life and marriage, and that his condition had been caused, or at least worsened, by his relationship with her. In September she made the thirty-hour journey from Berlin to Zürau. He was resolute, but very conscious of the pain he caused her: 'I am quite without feeling . . . I have committed the wrong for which she is tortured and furthermore I operate the instrument of torture' (T. 21.9.'17). In December they met for the last time in Prague, and after seeing her off on the train to Berlin, he went to

Kafka with his sister Ottla in Zürau

Zürau

Brod in his office and collapsed in tears. Since he felt that his illness was only a symptom of his inability to marry, he could not regard it as the cause of his action, but only as an excuse. He wrote to Ottla at this time that his illness was only outwardly the reason for breaking off the engagement.* His doubts about marriage had never been overcome, he had simply tried to forget them. Now he felt that fate had decided for him: he must, to avoid speedy self-destruction, withdraw from the battle with life and concentrate on his writing, his vocation and his curse. This brought some sense of relief.

Kafka heard little of Felice's subsequent life. She married a Berlin businessman in March 1919 and bore him two sons. The family fled to Switzerland and then to the United States in the 1930s, and Felice died there in 1960. She retained many of Kafka's letters and revealed something of that business sense which he had admired in her when she sold this correspondence to a publisher in 1955.

During his time in Zürau, from September 1917 to June 1918, Kafka experienced relative peace. His illness had relieved him of much responsibility; it encouraged laziness and justified his inability to lead a normal life. Thus he could say that he clung to it for comfort as a child clings to its mother's skirts (BR. 161). He spent eight hours of the day stretched out on a chair and often did not even bother to read. He knew that his condition was probably incurable, but this did not worry him too much. In the country folk around him he saw men who accepted life as it was, true 'citizens of the earth, protected against all insecurity

* K. Wagenbach, *F. Kafka*, Hamburg, 1964, p. 110.

and worry until their blissful death' (т. 8.10.'17), and their peace had a beneficial effect upon him. Daily life on the farm and in the village was a natural round of birth and joy, suffering and death, which he contrasted with city existence and the war. At this time he took a great interest in Tolstoy's ideas on natural existence. He was attracted by the image of his uncle Siegfried, the country doctor, happy in his simple life, although Kafka knew that he was closer to the country doctor of his own story of that title, isolated from the community. As always he could dream of justifying his peculiarity through his writing. But Kafka's literary aims were utopian: 'to raise the world into the pure, the true, the immutable' (т. 25.9.'17). Furthermore his mind was still divided. He wanted to recover, and to come to terms with his abnormality. His spiritual predicament seemed to him to be incapable of solution. There remained only various means of escaping from it or avoiding the issues, 'ways-out' as he called them, echoing the ape of *A Report to an Academy*. What appealed to him most at this time was to admit publicly his inability to cope with life (вr. 194 f.). Yet the desire to prove himself within the community was still strong: 'I strive to know the whole human and animal community, to recognize their basic predilections, desires, moral ideals, to reduce these to simple rules so that I may suit my behaviour to these rules and find favour in the eyes of the whole world' (т. 28.9.'17). In this context the goal of marriage could not be dismissed altogether.

In Zürau Kafka re-wrote, or reinterpreted, three well-known stories or legends, *Die Wahrheit über Sancho Panza* (*The Truth about Sancho Panza*), *Das Schweigen der Sirenen* (*The Silence of the Sirens*) and *Prometheus*. A similar piece, *Poseidon*, followed two years later. He saw Sancho Panza as one who escaped destruction and found amusement by directing his imagination or his desires, represented by Don Quixote, into spheres that had no connection with reality. The story of Odysseus and the Sirens also became an example of how to avoid destruction, through ingenuity or ignorance. For since the Sirens' song could not fail to lure a man to his death despite all his precautions, writes Kafka, the truth of the matter must be that the sirens did not sing (their silence was really even more dangerous than their song), and that Odysseus was ignorant of this, or pretended ignorance and thus deceived fate. Of Prometheus's eternal punishment Kafka wrote: 'The legend tried to explain the inexplicable. As it came out of a substratum of truth it had in turn to end in the inexplicable.' This comment might well serve as a motto for Kafka's own works. Poseidon he saw as a bureaucrat who has no time to view the seas that he administers. These brief reinterpretations or inversions of myth have encouraged critics to look for reapplications of legends in Kafka's major works. There are many possibilities of this kind. The central episode of *A Country Doctor*, for instance, in which the doctor is put naked into bed with his patient, recalls Flaubert's *St Julien l'Hospitalier*; in the legend as re-told by Flaubert the saint lies naked with a leper as a sign of penitence and love and is duly rewarded by transfiguration. Kafka reverses this: his doctor is forcibly undressed by the patient's family, finishing in a hell.

Many of Kafka's works have been called myths or parables, and many do, indeed, appear to be truths or ideas translated into narrative form. One of the most typical of these 'parables', pregnant with possible meanings, is *Eine alltägliche Verwirrung (An Everyday Confusion)*, also written in Zürau. It is based on the concept of subjective time and distance which plays a part in several of his stories. One man is so eager to reach an agreement with another that in his impatience he fails to make contact with him.

'All human errors are impatience' is the beginning of one of the aphoristic reflections Kafka wrote in Zürau. Just over one hundred in number, they were given the title *Betrachtungen über Sünde, Leid, Hoffnung und den wahren Weg (Reflections on Sin, Suffering, Hope and the True Way)* by Brod. With his illness confirmed, Kafka evidently felt that it was time to take stock. These aphorisms are concerned with problems similar to those found in his stories, but they translate them into more definitely religious terms. It is, however, not always clear whether the religious vocabulary is used to describe purely religious affairs or is employed metaphorically. Many of these strikingly compressed observations are no less opaque than his most puzzling stories; they are concerned with paradox and ambivalence in life, thought and language. Some are tinged by a wry casuistic humour or end with an ironic shrug of the shoulders. Several seem applicable to the novels and stories. 'It is only our conception of time that makes us call the Last Judgement by that name. It is in fact a kind of martial law' has been linked with *The Trial*; and 'There is a goal, but no way' could apply to *Before the Law* or *The Castle*. Pessimistic and despairing comments are balanced by statements which at least allow the possibility of ultimate truth and happiness:

> Only here is suffering suffering. Not in such a way as if those who suffer here were because of this suffering to be elevated elsewhere, but in such

a way that what in this world is called suffering, in another world, unchanged and only liberated from its opposite, is bliss. Expulsion from Paradise is in its main part eternal: it is final to be sure, life in the world is inescapable, but the eternity of the process (or expressed in temporal terms: the eternal repetition of the process) makes it nevertheless possible that we could not only remain for ever in Paradise, but actually be there all the time, whether we know it or not.

Another comment illustrates the mystical side of Kafka: 'There is no need for you to leave the house. Stay at your table and listen. Don't even listen, just wait. . . . The world will offer itself to you to be unmasked, it can't do otherwise, in raptures it will writhe before you.' There are also pronouncements that reflect his rigorous moral attitude and cold reasoning:

Everything is deception: seeking the minimum of illusion, keeping within the normal limitations, seeking the maximum. In the first case one cheats the Good, by trying to make it too easy for oneself to get it, and the Evil by imposing all too unfavourable conditions of warfare on it. In the second case one cheats the Good by not striving for it even in earthly terms. In the third case one cheats the Good by keeping as aloof from it as possible, and the Evil by hoping to make it powerless through intensifying it to the utmost. What would therefore seem to be preferable is the second case, for the Good is always cheated, and in this case, or at least to judge by appearance, the Evil is not cheated.

Kafka had not lost his interest in possible social solutions to inequality and unhappiness. In February 1918, at Zürau, he drew up in a notebook a plan for a community of workers without possessions. It would be confined, initially, to unmarried men, five hundred at the most. They would possess only simple clothing, enough to feed themselves, the equipment necessary for their work, and books. Payment for work would provide only the necessities of life. They must live moderately, share the lives of the poorest people, and nourish themselves on bread, water and dates – an indication that Kafka was probably thinking of Palestine. Hours of work would be restricted to six a day, four or five for heavy manual labour. Any previous possessions would be surrendered and the proceeds used to erect state hospitals and homes in which they would be cared for free of charge in illness or old age. The community would answer moral and spiritual problems; work would be a matter of conscience and an expression of belief in one's fellow men.

Kafka was fighting for the connection between his existence and the community, and the community to which he belonged, even as an outsider, was that of Prague. Despite his antipathy towards the city he was drawn back to it as to a challenge. In June 1918 his leave ended and he returned to the office. Despite continuing insomnia he had put on weight and was considered fit for work. But Zürau had not brought a complete release from anxiety. One night spent listening to the antics of mice in his room had reduced him to trembling terror which he hardly knew whether to laugh or cry about. His illness made him even more secretive than before. He kept his parents ignorant of his condition; for some time they believed that he was simply suffering from general debility.

During the summer and autumn of 1918 he spent his mornings in the office and his afternoons working as a gardener. The end of the war brought external changes; his office work had now to be conducted in Czech. But essentially his life was not changed. In November he began another five months of 'convalescence', this time in a private hotel in Schelesen (Zelizy), a small town north of Prague, and returned there late in 1919. Again Kafka avoided an orthodox sanatorium, and once more he was tempted to satisfy the demands of 'life'. In Schelesen he met Julie Wohryzek, to whom he became briefly engaged.

Kafka's father had approved of Felice Bauer, but was strongly opposed to this engagement, for the girl's father had neither money nor social standing. Hermann Kafka told his son he would do better to visit a brothel. The relationship between them had worsened, particularly since Kafka had supported Ottla in her bid for independence, and it reached one of its crisis points now, in November 1919, when Kafka wrote the remarkable *Letter to My Father*.

Kafka's feeling towards Julie Wohryzek seems scarcely to have been a burning passion, but in many respects his thoughts were probably very similar to those which occupied him during his affair with Felice Bauer. His description of Julie Wohryzek in a letter to Brod suggests that he did not expect intellectual companionship from her, but equally did not envisage her interfering with his creative writing. She was, he wrote, mad about the cinema, operettas and comedies, about powder and veils, she made incessant use of an inexhaustible stock of the cheekiest slang expressions, and was, on the whole, a very ignorant, jolly person. The most one could say of her position in society and among the racial groups was that she belonged to the nation of clerks. Yet she was basically plucky, reliable, unselfish – great qualities in a creature who was physically not without beauty, but really quite insignificant – as insignificant, he wrote, as the mosquito that flew against his lamp (BR. 252). He believed that for him this would be a marriage of common sense. His father's opposition only made him more determined to marry as quickly as possible. Yet a plan to marry hurriedly in November 1917 came to nothing; the outward obstacle was a failure to find a suitable place to live, but more decisive was Kafka's fear that marriage was incompatible with writing. The engagement stood for some months, but he had dismissed the prospect of a wedding.

Julie Wohryzek was about thirty years old when Kafka met her in Schelesen. In the winter of 1919, in that same town, which was a favourite holiday centre for the Jews of Prague, he came to know a younger girl, Minze E. She was then nineteen, a convalescent, and in poor spirits. He adopted a paternal attitude towards her and followed her subsequent career with interest. From his letters to her (hers are not extant and little is known of her, not even her full name) it appears that she was Jewish and interested in literature. He advised her that her spiritual predicament could be remedied by dedication to practical work, and it seems that over the next three years, during which she took up horticultural work and found a husband, she did begin to come to terms with life. Kafka's experience enabled him to sympathize with her troubles, and he inclined to think that no one, least of all someone still young, should succumb to despair.

Kafka returned to Prague in December 1919 and remained there until the following April. Once more, as in 1917, a significant defeat, or an escape from the threat of marriage, was followed by a period of stocktaking, recorded in aphoristic statements which often echo those written in Zürau.

These observations written in the first two months of 1920 contain few signs of religious faith. Only with great reservation may they be taken as pointers to the author's beliefs, although they certainly express his preoccupations. Brod gave this series the title *Er* (*He*), and most describe the thoughts and feelings of an unspecified person. This 'he' may often be Kafka himself, or part of his personality. As in his correspondence with Felice Bauer, Kafka here attributes his failures to the division of his self: 'He is thirsty and is cut off from a spring by a mere clump of bushes. But he is divided against himself: one part overlooks the whole, sees that he is standing here and that the spring is just beside him; but another part notices nothing, has at most a divination

that the first part sees all. But as he notices nothing he cannot drink.'
In another entry Kafka describes the struggle within the self as one
between two active participants, with a third person who is the passive
victim and yet is able to pass judgement on the other two. Such statements warn against too facile an identification of Kafka with the 'he'
in such entries as: 'Some deny the existence of misery by pointing to
the sun; he denies the existence of the sun by pointing to misery.'
Nor can we be sure whether this 'he' is regarded with pride or with
pity.

Early in 1920 Kafka became acquainted with a seventeen-year-old
schoolboy, Gustav Janouch, the son of a Czech colleague in the
insurance office. The boy's home life was unhappy. Like Minze E., he
found a substitute father in Kafka, who was able to give him advice
without appearing to condescend. The young Janouch, who had literary
aspirations, was thrilled to meet the author of *The Metamorphosis*, was
fascinated by his personality and worshipped his every word. Kafka
was apprehensive lest his pessimism should infect an impressionable
soul, and emphasized the distance which age and his illness placed
between them; but he was drawn to someone who reminded him of
his own youth and who was in need of help. While he was in Prague
and able to lead a relatively normal life he gave quite generously of his
time to Janouch – usually during office hours. Janouch noted Kafka's
words and gestures in his diaries, and twenty years later, after the
Second World War, he edited and published his record of his conversations with Kafka. It would be surprising if Janouch's memory did
not deceive him in matters of detail, yet his account is remarkably
convincing, and was accepted by Brod as a true picture of his friend.
Kafka's utterances in these conversations often recall in style and theme
the aphoristic thoughts and laconic reflections of his diaries and notebooks. In these meetings with Janouch he appears as a reserved man
with a melancholy smile who had a poor opinion of mankind but great
faith in human potentiality. For one so obsessed with himself he was
remarkably well informed, about not only the latest manifestations in
the world of literature and art, but also the political events of the
time. Despite a tendency to interpret all human affairs according to a
system of personal associations, he revealed an almost uncanny insight
into many matters as well as a rare gift of succinct expression. One
almost prophetic utterance, occasioned by the sight of a demonstration
of Czech workers, was characteristically developed by means of
metaphor:

Kafka said, 'These people are so self-possessed, so self-confident and good-humoured. They rule the streets, and therefore think they rule the world. In fact, they are mistaken. Behind them already are the secretaries, officials, professional politicians, all the modern satraps for whom they are preparing the way to power.'

'You do not believe in the power of the masses?'

'It is before my eyes, this power of the masses, formless and apparently chaotic, which then seeks to be given a form and a discipline. At the end of every truly revolutionary development there appears a Napoleon Bonaparte.'

'You don't believe in the wider expansion of the Russian Revolution?'

Kafka was silent for a moment, then he said: 'As a flood spreads wider and wider, the waters become shallower and dirtier. The Revolution evaporates, and leaves behind only the slime of a new bureaucracy. The chains of tormented mankind are made out of red tape' (J. 80).

Max Brod has stated that in company Kafka was usually composed, and referred to Janouch's record as corroborative evidence. For most of these conversations with Janouch took place while Kafka was experiencing a great emotional upheaval, a love affair which surpassed his previous involvements in intensity and caused him to break with Julie Wohryzek.

Heights and depths

In April 1920 Kafka began another three months' sick leave, this time in Merano in the South Tyrol. There he was amused and disturbed by German guests at the same hotel who, puzzled by his accent and challenged by his reticence, tried to establish his provenance and exhibited various degrees of embarrassed condescension and hostility towards him as a Jew. From Merano he began his second great correspondence with a woman, letters which in their frankness are comparable to those addressed to Felice Bauer, but surpass them in self-knowledge and succinct (often cryptic) expression.

The recipient of these letters was instinctively attuned to his manner of thought. Gifted with intelligence and intuition, she was convinced of his genius and could converse with him on equal terms about his main preoccupations. Milena Jesenská-Polak was also the only woman loved by Kafka who was a public figure, well-known in social and literary circles in Prague and Vienna. In some ways she belonged to a different world: she was not a Jew, came from an old, respected Czech family with nationalist leanings, was twelve years younger than he, and full of self-confidence, determination and energy. Yet the two had much in common. Like him she had suffered greatly in her emotional life, and was tormented by feelings of love and hate for a tyrannical

A page from a letter to Milena

father. Her mother had died when Milena was thirteen, and her wilful father, Jan Jesensky, a successful dentist and professor in Prague, had little time for his daughter. She and her friends at an élite girls' school indulged their fantasies in defying the standards of their parents, they visited cemeteries at night and swam the river Moldau fully clothed. Milena frequented the literary and artistic circles of Prague and earned a reputation as a colourful character, an emancipated young woman who worshipped feeling and flaunted convention, was extravagant with her money and her affections and expected similar generosity from others. She fell in love with Oskar Polak, an intelligent Jew of Bohemian habits, an 'eternal student' and a lady-killer, who met with her father's wholehearted disapproval. To combat her obstinate attachment to Polak, he sent his daughter to a psychiatric institution, but she fled from this virtual prison and married Polak in 1918. Her father disowned her, and the couple went to live in Vienna. Polak neglected Milena and had other love affairs, and she was forced to look for work to support them both. She found occasional employment, as a railway porter and a teacher, and wrote articles on Viennese life, fashion and literature for Czech papers and magazines. She began to translate contemporary German authors, including Kafka, into Czech, and it was through this that she came to know Kafka, who had in fact met her before in Prague though he hardly remembered her. She was now twenty-four, but an experienced woman of the world. Some twenty years later, after she had left Polak, she became a Communist and was interned by the Nazis. In the concentration camp, an ill woman, she was an imposing figure among her fellow prisoners. She died there in 1944, after an unsuccessful kidney operation.

Kafka was not just flattered by her admiration for his work, he was overwhelmed and frightened. In a letter to her he compared his feelings with those he imagined to have been felt by Dostoyevsky when one night the writer Gregorovich and the critic Nekrasov called on the novelist to proclaim him a genius: 'Dostoyevsky, who always referred to this night as the happiest of his life, leans against the window, follows them with his eyes, is quite beside himself and begins to cry. . . . His basic feeling . . . was: "These wonderful people! How good and noble they are! And how base am I!"' (BrM. 18). The power of her personality, and the strength of her feelings, filled him with awe and apprehension. He described her in a letter to Brod as a living fire such as he had never seen before (Br. 275). A flood of letters and telegrams from her met with a cautious response. As before with Felice Bauer, he welcomed someone in whom he could confide, but was anxious to maintain his position of isolation: 'I can't listen simultaneously to the terrible voice from within and to you, but I can listen to the former and entrust it to you, to you, as to no one else in the world' (BrM. 43). Yet Milena must have made much of her own troubles, her relationship with her father, her marital problems, her material insecurity and her lack of health, knowing that he would be attracted to a sister soul. Her letters to him have never been made public. It seems that she wooed him instinctively, not from coquetry, but from a belief in her love for him. She had an unusual empathy towards him. He saw her as a danger, threatening a renewal of the conflicts from which he had hoped to escape when his illness was diagnosed. Moreover it now seemed too late to come to terms with 'life' and to make a meaningful contact with another person. But he wished to help her and to see her happy. Thus he suggested that he could support her financially if she left her husband, and planned to develop his relations with her from afar. Yet, after weeks of resistance, Kafka agreed to return to Prague via Vienna. On 24 June 1920 they met in Vienna and spent four intoxicated days together. They walked all day over the hills behind the city, he ate enormous meals, slept like a log, and did not cough once. She later told Brod that Kafka forgot his *Angst* for these few days, and that his illness meant no more to them than a slight cold (Brod. 286).

On his return to Prague he spent his afternoons in the office, waiting for a letter from Milena. He poured out his exuberant feelings to Brod. Fearing that an emotional crisis would have disastrous effects on Kafka's health, Brod warned Milena to handle his friend with the utmost care, and urged Kafka to give up the office and retire to a sanatorium. The future was by no means clear. Kafka now broke finally with Julie Wohryzek, though not without protracted embarrassment. He realized that Milena's jealous scorn of Julie was unjust, and did not wish to hurt his fiancée more than was necessary. A few years later she was to be admitted to a mental home, where she probably died.

There is no reason to suppose that Kafka regarded marriage to Milena with unambiguous enthusiasm. Milena, for her part, did not wish to leave her husband, still perhaps hoping that a generous attitude on her part might restore their relationship (and, indeed, when Polak learnt of her affair with Kafka he became more interested in her again). Later Milena admitted that she feared the life of asceticism which Kafka would have demanded of her. Besides, she was convinced that he did not have long to live. Kafka was probably happy that the decision lay with her. A second meeting of the lovers in the summer of 1920, in the town of Gmünd on the Austrian–Czechoslovak border, lasted a few hours only and was a disaster. He could not bring himself at this decisive moment to play the lover and live only for the present. Milena was ready to live with him for a while, but not to marry him; such plans did not satisfy his longing for purity and his hatred of half-measures. Yet it was the very lack of need to think about the future that filled him with happiness in those moments when he was able to surrender to his love. He wrote that both of them were indissolubly married – he to his *Angst* – and that they should never again talk of the future, only of the present (BRM. 197). His present had been filled by Milena: 'Either the world is so tiny or we are so enormous, in any case we fill it completely' (BRM. 89). Even in his moments of deepest despair he felt that she could understand him. Indeed, Milena helped him to define his *Angst* and diagnosed his condition with unique insight; she wrote to Brod:

> We are all capable of living because at some time or other we took refuge in lies, in blindness, in enthusiasm, in optimism, in some conviction or other, in pessimism or something of that sort. But he never escaped to any such sheltering refuge, none at all. . . . He possesses not the slightest refuge. For that reason he is exposed to all those things against which we are protected. (Brod. 281)

Yet she was amazed by his refusal to contemplate a *mariage à trois* and thought his standards those of a saint.

After the meeting at Gmünd they continued to correspond, although both of them knew that their relationship had no future. In the autumn he suggested that they should write no more, but it was not until the winter that he himself complied with this suggestion. From a sanatorium to which he retired in December 1920 he wrote a desperate plea to be left alone which caused Milena to contact Brod: 'I simply don't know what to do. . . . Only tell me this one thing – you must know, you were with him lately: am I at fault or am I not at fault? . . . I want to know whether I am the kind of person who has made Frank suffer the way he has suffered from every other woman so that his sickness has grown worse . . .' (Brod. 284). She recovered from her bewilderment and despair and visited Kafka in Prague several times in 1921 and again the next year. They wrote to each other occasionally until his death. He trusted her with his innermost secrets. He gave her his diaries and some manuscripts which she retained until his death, when she passed them to Brod.

Prague, the Troya staircase

His attitude towards Milena was coloured by a conviction which had not been so pronounced in his feelings for Felice Bauer and which can be only partly explained by his illness: the belief that he was unclean and was dragging the woman down into the filth in which he lived. Such self-abasement hid his yearning for the miraculous – for Milena to divorce Polak and marry him. This dream seemed the ultimate in presumption, for he nourished an unshakeable respect for Polak's worth as a man. Accused by Milena of being incapable of love, he replied that this confirmed his image of himself:

> It's more or less like this: I, an animal of the forest . . . lay somewhere in a dirty ditch (dirty only as a result of my being there, of course). Then I saw you outside in the open – the most wonderful thing I'd ever seen. I forgot everything entirely, forgot myself, got up, came closer – though fearful in this new yet familiar freedom – came closer nevertheless, reached you, you were so good, I cowered beside you, as though it were my right, laid my face in your hand, I was so happy, so proud, so free, so powerful, so at home. . . . This could not last. . . . I had experienced the dream-fright of behaving as though one were at home in a place where one does not belong. This fright I experienced in reality, I had to return to the darkness. . . . I was desperate, really like a stray animal, I began to run . . . (BrM. 223 f.)

This affair with a Christian woman caused him to ponder again on what it meant to be a Jew. When he heard anti-Semitic outbursts in the street he felt that he was a fraud in the security of his position in the office. Seeing a crowd of destitute Jewish refugees from eastern Europe waiting for permission to emigrate to America, he longed to be one of them. Anti-Semitic propaganda taught that a Jew defiled everything that he touched, and at some moments Kafka believed that this was true of himself. He wrote to Milena: 'We both know enough typical examples of western Jews, I am as far as I know the most typical western Jew among them. This means, expressed with exaggeration, that not one calm moment is granted me, nothing is granted me, everything has to be earned, not only the present and the future, but the past too' (BrM. 247). But resignation gave him dignity, and the thought of his own mortality made him tolerant of weaknesses in himself and others. In the autumn of 1920 he wrote to Milena of a Chinese story in which a wise man on his deathbed is ridiculed by a young follower for always speaking of death, but never dying. The wise man replied that some men's last words last longer than others. Kafka comments: 'This is true, and it is unjust to smile about the hero who lies mortally wounded on the stage and sings an aria. We lie on the ground and sing for years' (BrM. 239).

The letters to Milena betray an inner tension. Without a knowledge of her replies our insight into the affair is limited, but it is clear that Kafka's tendency to fluctuate in mood, from despair to euphoria, from emotional sterility to intense feeling, was by now very marked. This development was, no doubt, connected with the progress of his illness. Abrupt changes of mood, characteristic of all his writings, are particularly apparent in some of the sketches he wrote in this autumn of 1920.

Once more the pattern was repeated: a short period of creativity following an intense emotional experience and a withdrawal, voluntary or forced, into isolation. Now he was copying out and ordering the earlier aphorisms, to which he seems to have attached some importance, and entering more such observations into his notebooks. None of the sketches and fragments written late in 1920 were considered worthy of publication by their author. They vary in tone from dramatic horror to bemused or whimsical detachment. Many represent variations on earlier themes, particularly those of the *Great Wall of China*. In *Nachts (At Night)* a man watches while others sleep, but to no known purpose; there is an evident connection with Kafka's insomnia and nocturnal writing. Alienation and isolation are expressed in *Heimkehr (Home-Coming)*; helplessness in *Der Steuermann (The Helmsman)*; impotence and ignorance in *Die Abweisung (Rejection)* and *Zur Frage der Gesetze (The Problem of Our Laws)*. In *Das Stadtwappen (The City Coat of Arms)* Kafka comments on the Tower of Babel, never completed because men were more concerned to create a comfortable home on earth than to reach up to Heaven. A notebook entry, probably made a few months later, mentions the Pit of Babel, suggesting that man's efforts to reach out to the heavens are totally misconceived and futile (H. 387). We may, perhaps, understand that he blamed the fate of mankind on materialism, and his own supposed failure as a writer on his inability to sever all ties with 'life'. Personal and universal, worldly and religious considerations are interwoven in these sketches as in his more famous works. One parable from this period may be quoted to illustrate Kafka's ability to sum up in an image and with a minimum of words his darkly humourous reaction to absurdity; this piece also shows how Kafka's writings allow many possible interpretations, for it will mean different things to different people, depending on their experience:

Little Fable
'Alas,' said the mouse, 'the world is growing smaller every day. At the beginning it was so big that I was afraid, I kept running and running, and I was glad when at last I saw walls far away to the right and left, but these long walls have narrowed so quickly that I am in the last chamber already, and there in the corner stands the trap that I must run into.' 'You only need to change your direction,' said the cat, and ate it up.

Even more forceful in its assault upon the emotions is *Der Geier* (*The Vulture*), with its horror and intoxication with pain: the narrator is being hacked to pieces by a vulture, and then, just as help is promised, he is killed, but experiences a profound sense of release. Humiliation and bewilderment are reflected in *Die Truppenaushebung* (*The Conscription of the Troops*) where those who are willing to sacrifice all to undertake an unknown and dangerous task are rejected, but the majority of spiritless subjects enlisted for service. Paradox is the essence of *Die Prüfung* (*The Test*) too, another more cerebral piece written in a detached, bemused style: a man who is a servant yet is never given a job to do, who regards himself as a failure, is asked questions that he cannot understand, let alone answer, only to be told that he has passed the test. Has he proved himself by his humility and willingness to admit ignorance? Does success in the test of life require the abdication of reason? Kafka was a master of the art of raising questions and propounding problems in a few lines.

During the war Kafka had compared his inner conflict with the efforts of the soldiers at the front, and in the autumn of 1920 he called his life 'military service' and 'life on manoeuvres' (BrM. 208). Once again he had taken to sleeping in the afternoon and writing at night. Not surprisingly, his health was deteriorating rapidly. Brod's constant exhortations and his own longing for a cure caused him to make enquiries about sanatoria. But none of those he contacted, near Vienna, seemed suitable. Brod's wife obtained a residence permit from the Austrian authorities on his behalf. Finally Kafka's sister Ottla took matters in hand, made arrangements for him to be granted further leave from the office and booked him into a Czech sanatorium. She was familiar with his reluctance to face practical matters and his inability to take decisions, knew that he needed to break completely with Milena and probably advised him to stop writing to her. So in December 1920 Kafka, accompanied by Ottla, set off, not south-east towards Vienna, but east to the High Tatra mountains of Slovakia. There, in a sanatorium at Matliary, he remained for nine months.

The Matlárháza in Tatranske, Matliary, where Kafka stayed from December 1920 to late summer 1921

Kafka informed Brod that it was a pleasant place, particularly since the sanatorium was also a hotel with normal healthy guests. He dared not hope for any improvement in his condition. He envied the sanatorium's doctor his conviction that all his ills could be attributed to consumption and could all be remedied by a course of injections. Yet outwardly he was an exemplary patient, stretched in a deckchair on his balcony, a thermometer in his mouth, thankful that the building was not over-full, and therefore quiet, and enjoying the peace, waiting for the altitude and the fresh air to work upon his body. But inwardly he was not at ease. Milena was still on his mind. Furthermore he saw the other patients tortured by illness, and more horribly, by the medical treatment. One evening brought a traumatic experience. Out of kindness he visited a fellow patient, a Czech of about fifty, who could not leave his room. This man showed him a system of mirrors with which he had to direct the rays of the sun into his own infected throat. Kafka almost fainted and left the room hurriedly. He did not sleep much that night. What he had seen was to him worse than an execution, worse than physical torture – 'this torture lasts for years, with artificial pauses to drag it out, and – most characteristic – the tortured man is forced to prolong the torture himself, of his own free will, from within his wretched self. This wretched life in bed, the fever, difficult breathing, taking medicines, the painful and dangerous use of mirrors (he can easily burn himself if he is at all clumsy), it all has no other purpose than to prolong as long as possible this wretched life, fever, etc., by slowing down the growths which must eventually suffocate him' (BR. 294).

By now Kafka had almost ready-made answers to Brod's persistent enquiries about his *Angst*: 'You underline "fear of what". Of so much, but on the worldly level above all it is fear that I do not suffice, bodily or spiritually, to carry the weight of another person. . . . You write "Why be more afraid of love than of anything else in life?" and just before that "In love I have come closest, very frequently, to experiencing the divine." With these two sentences together you might as well say "Why not fear every bush as much as the burning bush?" ' (BR. 297). Yet he felt that he could not really explain himself.

His health did not improve, and often he felt incapable of writing letters; he had no energy and believed that he was already dozing his life away like an old man. Yet he was able to forget his physical condition in frequent conversations about literature and Jewish thought with a student of medicine who was both a T.B. patient and a medical assistant in the sanatorium. This man, Robert Klopstock, a Jew from Budapest but of Czech parentage, was then twenty-one years old. Kafka took a paternal, or avuncular, interest in him, much as in his relations with Minze E. and Gustav Janouch. Over the next few years he went to some trouble to help Klopstock, who seems to have been rather lost and aimless, and even, after his return to Prague, wrestled with the Czech authorities to procure a passport for him, a tiresome exercise which he would not have undertaken on his own behalf.

In March 1921 Kafka asked Brod to arrange for his sick leave to be extended. The doctors advised that another few months of treatment would bring recovery. He had put on weight, but was otherwise no better in health, and did not expect any improvement. He was reluctant to give details of his condition, but when Brod sent him a questionnaire to be completed he complied with characteristic humour; the reply reads: 'Weight gained: 8 kg. Total weight: over 65 kg. Objective condition of lungs: the doctor's secret, apparently favourable. Respiration: not good, on cold evenings almost as in winter. Signature: the only question that embarrasses me' (BR. 338). In his desperate state his wildest dreams were quite modest: his ideal was reasonable health,

A picture postcard from Matliary, sent to his parents

and the opportunity to work at a trade in a southern land. In May it was the turn of Ottla and her husband to request further extension of leave for him. In September he returned to Prague and to the office.

He was still subject to bouts of coughing, to headaches, digestive problems, and insomnia. Often he had to retire to bed as soon as he had finished the morning's work in the office. Brief visits from Minze E. and Milena were a strain. He felt guilty about the amount of leave he had taken and was reluctant to ask for more. Yet in January 1922 he began another four weeks' sick leave, which he spent at Spindelmühle in the Bohemian Riesengebirge.

Although under medical supervision in Spindelmühle he did not spare his body, but engaged in winter sports. He said that he had decided to invite a quick death by exhausting his remaining energies. To Brod he wrote how he wished that his friend could join him for just a few days, they would climb all day long, toboggan, and possibly even ski – so far he had taken only five steps – and they would write, and thus accelerate the inevitable, but peaceful end (BR. 370). Several times since leaving Matliary he had thought death very near. In the winter he had started to make 'final' observations on his life:

> I have never, for any lasting period of time, given my life the slightest direction. It was as if I, like everyone else, had been given the centre of a circle and I had, like every other man, to go along the decisive radius and describe the beautiful circle. Instead whenever I started along a radius I always had to break off (examples: piano, violin, languages, German studies, anti-Zionism, Zionism, Hebrew, gardening, carpentry, writing, attempts at marriage, own apartment). The centre of my imaginary circle bristles with the beginnings of radii, there is no room for a new start, no room means old age, weak nerves, and no new start means the end. If I once progressed a little further than usual along a radius, as with the study of law or with my engagements, everything was worse rather than better, and precisely by that amount. (T. 23.1.'22)

After a wintry excursion in Spindelmühle he feared that he would fall a victim to pneumonia. Probably at that time he wrote a note, not found until after his death, instructing Brod to destroy his manuscripts. Brod had suspected that his friend was suffering from a persecution mania while in Matliary, and Kafka himself was now more than ever aware that he was on the verge of insanity. He was quick to attribute any annoyance to evil spirits conspiring against him. He had not ceased to regard his urge to write as part of his illness, which rest and medical treatment had failed to cure or even to arrest in its inevitable progress. If then the enemy could not be beaten, why not 'mount your attacker's horse and ride it yourself'? (T. 9.3.'22). Since returning from Matliary he had tried not to lead the life of a recluse, and had begun to write again. In March, after the short stay at Spindelmühle, he read the beginning of *The Castle* to Brod. In May he sent the manuscript of *Erstes Leid* (*First Sorrow*) to the publisher Kurt Wolff. It is not clear whether this renewed literary activity represented a surrender to an all-powerful urge, or was undertaken in heroic defiance of fate. Kafka knew that writing brought him suffering as well as satisfaction. In October 1921 he had written that anything he might write about Milena would be aimed too directly against himself (T. 15.10.'21). Yet *The Castle*, on which he was working for the greater part of 1922, had as much (and as little) to do with Milena as *The Trial* with Felice.

In January he had entered in his diary: 'Remarkable, mysterious, maybe dangerous, maybe redeeming consolation of writing. . . . A higher kind of observation is created, higher, not keener, and the higher it is . . . the more it becomes independent, the more it follows its own laws of movement, the more incalculable, the more joyful, the more ascendant its path' (T. 27.1.'22). *First Sorrow* shows a trapeze artist dedicated to his solitary task, obeying rules that apply only to him; he rises above others in his strange pursuit, but he also succumbs to its inherent danger. He tells his manager that in future he must have two trapeze bars, not just one. The manager agrees, but is shaken by the emotion shown by the artist. For the first time the artist's brow, as smooth as a child's, is furrowed by suffering, by worries which the manager realizes must threaten the artist's very existence. The artist sobs that he cannot live with just one bar in his hands.

Kafka has taken literally the phrase '*einen Halt im Leben haben*', to have a hold, a firm basis, in life, just as he had played with the word 'to ape' in *A Report to an Academy*. The artist's first, and possibly fatal, acquaintance with anxiety is made when he questions the adequacy of his one hold in (or on) life. He has come close to perfection in his difficult art, and has not been worried about the isolation it entails. But now he realises the precariousness of his situation. Ironically, two trapezes are unlikely to make his work any safer. The links with Kafka's view of his own position are clear. For years he had seen himself as a person apart, isolated and exposed. After his return to his parent's home from Matliary he noted that when his parents were playing cards he sat apart, a perfect stranger (T. 25.10.'21). In Spindelmühle he reflected on his position as an inhabitant of a different world to which he had been banished, or had banished himself. Kafka's isolation had several causes; the trapeze artist of *First Sorrow* isolates himself solely, it seems, for the sake of his art. He becomes the victim of anxiety and of discontent. Kafka noted that he himself had always been discontented, even with his own contentment (T. 24.1.'22). This brief story is told with ironic detachment and has touches of humour. The artist's bodily needs are attended to by a team of men who haul pots up and down on ropes, his journeys from one theatre to another are made in racing cars in the early hours of the morning, or on the luggage rack of a train. The artist's emotions seem childish, and the manager's reactions exaggerated:

> At that the trapeze artist suddenly burst into tears. Deeply distressed, the manager sprang to his feet and asked what was the matter, then getting no answer climed up on the seat and caressed him cheek to cheek, so that his own face was bedabbled by the trapeze artist's tears.

Kafka prepared this story for publication in a collection called *Ein*

Emil Nolde *Masks II* 1920

Hungerkünstler (*A Hunger Artist*) which appeared in 1924 and includes other stories that are concerned, at least on one level, with the fate of an artist. In a wider application it could refer to any actor in the theatre of life, who questions an assumption on which his 'performance' has been based.

A Hunger Artist, probably written a few weeks after *First Sorrow*, also tells of a performer who, because of his longing to perfect his art, is isolated from all others. He fasts for long periods. Once as a one-man show touring towns and cities he starved for set periods, forty days at a time, because his manager knew that public interest could not be sustained for longer. The artist was not happy. He was reluctant to accept this time limit, and perturbed that the public could not be convinced that he did not cheat. Indeed, onlookers were indifferent to his achievement and were entertained only by the showmanship attendant upon his act. Yet even this interest diminished and his one-

Max Ernst *The Horde* 1927

man show became unprofitable. Reluctantly but resignedly he took
employment in a circus, where he became a minor side show, no more
than an obstacle on the way to the menagerie. Eventually he is for-
gotten, but has the opportunity· to starve for a very long period.
Nobody records the number of days, and he is cheated of the satisfaction of measuring what he had achieved. One day he is discovered
dying. Circus managers and public have neglected him cruelly. Yet
with his dying breath the artist begs forgiveness of others. For he
confesses that he had expected their admiration, but that he had starved
only because no food appealed to him. If he had found palatable food he
would have eaten like anyone else. This human freak and his bed of
straw are removed from the cage, which is now used to house a
panther. The animal in its awesome vitality proves a much greater
public attraction. The grotesque and horrid tale is made bearable by
touches of humour.

The artist's dedication to the achievement of a superhuman feat arises from a fault in his human condition. His artistry is a fraud. It is a necessity for him, but in all other respects seems quite senseless. His claim to public esteem is based on a falsehood. His extraordinary feat gives him an insight into his own worthlessness. Yet does not his self-destructive performance give more cause for wonderment than the achievement of the monkey of *A Report to an Academy* who denies his true nature and copies others in order to survive? The story raises another question, which Kafka neither formulates nor answers: is the man at fault for not liking food, or is the world to blame for not providing it for him? The hunger artist's cage itself can be seen to symbolize not only imprisonment and deprivation, but also security, just as in his notebooks Kafka described his spiritual condition both as a striving to break out from and a desire to find a true home in the restriction of his 'cell'.

The story sheds some light on Kafka's wish that his work be destroyed. For him his writing was as private and as senseless as the superlative act of the hunger artist. It was not admirable since it resulted from his 'abnormality'. Doubts about the function of the artist have obsessed other modern writers, but none have been so tortured by these doubts as Kafka, and none have translated them into such a succinct or more profoundly ironic and unsettling vision.

The four months in Prague from March to June 1922, during which Kafka was working on these stories, various sketches and fragments, and continuing with *The Castle*, brought him a clearer realization that it was nonsensical to stay in the insurance company. At the end of June he applied for early retirement and a pension. This request was granted, although he made it in bad conscience, believing that he had cheated his employers over the past fourteen years. Immediately he left Prague and his parents' home to live once again with his sister Ottla, this time in Planá in south-eastern Bohemia.

Ottla was kind and considerate and his time in Planá relatively happy. The small town promised to be less frequented by holiday-makers than Spindelmühle, but Kafka was soon complaining of noise and used earplugs in vain. He shared a small house with Ottla, her husband and young child. Outside other children sometimes played noisily and a railway yard nearby produced raucous sounds at distressingly frequent intervals. The local children were augmented, to Kafka's horror, by a party on vacation from Prague. Furthermore he was obliged to return briefly to the city from which he had just escaped when his father fell seriously ill. Kafka was deeply moved, and hurt when his father showed little interest in him even at this time, when his son was looking for reconciliation.

Although he longed for isolation and quiet in which to work, Kafka needed human company and feared complete solitude. In September Ottla was to leave Planá; Kafka made plans to stay on alone, but regretted this immediately. Recognizing his panic reaction, Ottla resolved the difficulty with ease and cancelled the arrangements he had made. He explained his feelings to Brod.

> If I stay here on my own I shall be absolutely alone. . . . What does solitude mean? Basically solitude is my only goal, my greatest lure, my possibility, and presupposing that it can be said that I have 'arranged' my life at all, then I did so with the thought that solitude should be at home in it. And yet the fear of that which I love so much. Much more comprehensible is the anxiety to preserve solitude. . . . I am ground between these two fears. (br. 415)

When, in July, Oskar Baum invited Kafka to join him, Kafka had panicked for fear of losing his solitude. Furthermore, although Baum's offer of a quiet room seemed eminently sensible, Kafka was paralysed by an obsessive fear of change, 'fear that I would, by an action that is a great one by my standards, attract the attention of the gods'. (br. 384) In the letter to Brod which expresses this fear he linked the absolute claims of his art with the power of darkness:

> Last night I could not sleep and turned everything over between my aching temples, and once again I became conscious of something I had almost forgotten recently in my relative peace: what vulnerable or even nonexistent ground I live on, over darkness from which the dark power emerges whenever it likes and, without heeding my stammering, destroys my life. Writing preserves me, but is it not more correct to say that it preserves this kind of life? I do not of course mean that my life is better when I do not write. Rather it is much worse then, quite unbearable, bound to end in madness . . . a writer who does not write is of course an absurdity that provokes madness. But what does it mean to be a writer? Writing is a sweet, wonderful reward, but for what? Last night it became clear to me, with the clarity of a picture designed for the instruction of children, that it is the reward for service to the devil. This descent to the dark powers, this unchaining of spirits that are bound by nature, dubious embraces and whatever else goes on below. . . . Perhaps there is writing of a different kind, I know only this one: in the

night, when *Angst* prevents me from sleeping, I know only this one. And the devil's part in it seems very clear to me. (BR. 384 f.)

There may be a connection between this view of writing and Kafka's feelings about his father's illness; for he had seen his literary activity as an attempt to free himself from his father, who, at least in part, stood for what was normal and good. In writing, therefore, he had increased his guilt towards his father. Yet just as the father played an ambiguous role in his thoughts, so did writing. It was associated alternately with the heights and the depths. To Felice he had written that if anything about him was good it was the act of writing; and in the same month, June 1913, to Felice again, that writing had its being in the depths, while the office was up above in life, suggesting that writing was not only profounder, but also baser (BRF. 412 f.). In 1920 he wrote the phrase 'writing as a form of prayer' (H. 348), which has been much quoted by some interpreters of Kafka, but takes a new aspect in the light of the letter to Brod cited above.

The vacillations in Kafka's view of writing mirror his uncertainty. He greatly admired Thomas Mann's *Tonio Kröger* (1903), a story of the bad conscience of the alienated writer. Like Mann (whose *Dr Faustus* of 1947 is a full-scale treatment of this theme), but with greater personal involvement, he feared that genius involved a surrender to evil. Of one thing he was fairly clear: his earlier dreams of raising the world to 'the pure, the true, the immutable' now seemed misconceived. Writing had been necessary for him, it was his only possible mode of existence. It might therefore be said to be his means of salvation, but it might equally well be called his damnation. It stood apart from the world of normality and could not help others. This thought must have preyed on his mind when in conversation with Janouch, who recounts the following scene:

> Kafka placed his clenched fists on the table and said in a low, suppressed voice: 'One must be silent, if one can't give any help. No one, through his own lack of hope, should make the condition of the patient worse . . . I am no light . . . I'm a dead end.'
> Kafka leaned backwards. His hands slipped lifelessly from the table. He closed his eyes. (J. 202 f.)

We may link such despair with the decision, apparently reached early in September 1922 in Planá, to abandon *The Castle*. Kafka himself connected this decision with a psychological 'breakdown'. He experienced three such crises in Planá, occasioned by the noise of children playing, Baum's invitation, and the prospect of remaining alone.

It was probably at this time too that he laid aside *Forschungen eines Hundes* (*Investigations of a Dog*). In this story, as in *A Report to an Academy*, an animal explains his life, and this perspective gives rise to grotesque humour. The dog has become estranged from the canine community through his persistence in following up certain questions about life. He is fascinated by supernatural phenomena that might shed light on the mystery of life. His main investigations, however, concern the origin of nourishment, and perhaps therefore the basis of life itself. Dogs generally believe that food emanates from the earth, but he suspects that the sky plays an important part and undertakes an experiment, which involves fasting, in order to prove this to himself. The experiment is brought to a premature end by a hound who seems to have unearthly power. The dog discovers that it is probably impossible to find answers to his questions, and makes some observations on apparent contradictions in canine behaviour. In many ways this story reflects Kafka's position as an outsider concerned with existential problems. The canine community may perhaps be equated with the Jews or with mankind in general. Through the dog, Kafka examines, sceptically and ironically, the possibility of knowledge. The story reduces art and metaphysics to the level of absurd pantomine, it questions the validity of the sciences and of philosophies of history. Possibly its greatest irony lies in the dog's apparently complete ignorance of the existence of humans who could well be the providers of food. The dog is most amazed, not by miraculous events, but by the ability of other dogs to refrain from considering or talking about the problems that obsess him. The matter-of-fact hound refuses to recognize paradox; like the chaplain in *The Trial*, he seems to suggest that one must accept the world as it is. With an intellectual lucidity that distinguishes this monologue from his earlier dream-like stories, and with a more obvious delight in comic detail, Kafka portrays a character attempting to force the world to reveal its secrets. The narrator of *Investigations of a Dog* is a relative of the hero of *The Castle*.

Exclusion unto death

Discussions on the meaning and value of Kafka's work often focus on *The Castle*, his most ambitious and complex novel, written in 1922. Like *The Trial*, it confronts the reader who wishes to understand its every aspect with insuperable obstacles. We are told much of the hero's thoughts and feelings, but nothing of his background. We cannot be quite certain why he attempts to enter the castle, which itself is as mysterious as the court in *The Trial*, and which as a goal seems to contain a threat as well as a promise. Everything is told as the hero sees it, clearly or unclearly, in his moods of vexation, disappointment and weariness. In perspective and theme the novel is similar to *The Trial*, only here the hero is shown as an aggressor rather than a victim, and the society in which he moves and its members are depicted in greater detail. K.'s relationship with Frieda, in particular, has a dimension which was scarcely developed in the earlier novel, for the reader is almost able to identify with the girl as well as with the hero. The events, situations and conversations are never so far removed from normality, nor so fantastic as in *The Trial*. Yet the world of the novel is indeed strange – and terrible and oppressive to the hero; his experiences, if they do not have the totally horrific qualities of a nightmare, nevertheless display those of a dream in which frustration remorselessly

'The battered expressionist castle' from *The Chronicle of the Grey House* dir. Von Gerlach, 1925

engulfs almost every hope of success, and absurdity and normality are hopelessly confounded.

One evening K. arrives on foot in a village and claims that he is a land surveyor who has been engaged to work there by the count in the castle. There is some doubt about this claim: K. presents no written evidence, and two assistants, who, he says, will bring his instruments, never materialize. K. himself expects difficulties and resorts to subterfuge in order to gain acceptance as a surveyor. He sets out to do battle with the castle and its officials to this end, which itself is perhaps only a means to enter the castle. As the action progresses he is forced, at least temporarily, to lower his sights. He never relinquishes his claim to be a surveyor, but he is frustrated in his hopes of entering the castle or of meeting the secretary, Klamm, who is apparently responsible for the castle's dealings with him. At first he scorns contacts with lower officials, but eventually accepts a summons to an interview with an under-secretary, Erlanger, only to miss the appointment. He talks to another official, Bürgel, but is too tired and distraught to make anything of this opportunity to further his aims. A short meeting with Erlanger seems to bring him no advantage. What he learns from the village people about the castle is uncertain and sometimes contradictory. Most of the villagers regard him as a nuisance.

K. is an outsider in a society which is as inhospitable, from indifference or hostility, as the apparently eternal winter that reigns over the village. Frustration and exclusion find equally vivid expression in many incidents.

The castle itself is as unapproachable as the court in *The Trial*. Its higher officials live in a realm of mystery and seem to have no existence as individuals; they are interchangeable. The secretaries who frequent the village are said to be overworked, yet sleep much of the time. There are signs of muddle and incompetence. Paper work rules the lives of all the officials, and the village mayor is bound hand and foot by red tape. In the Herrenhof inn, where the castle bureaucrats live and work when visiting the village, K. witnesses a virtual *Papierkrieg* (paper-war or struggle with red tape) as files are distributed at dawn to secretaries and clerks in rooms on both sides of a long corridor. As strange and sinister as the bureaucracy is the attitude of the villagers to the castle. Although their knowledge of the castle is limited, they submit to its rules and believe it infallible. They look upon K. as a crazy troublemaker because he suspects the castle of incompetence, challenges the authority of its lesser representatives, and refuses to accept that no one but an official can gain entry to it. The village is in a sense at one with the authority that rules over it. K. is indeed told that there is no real difference between castle and village. One sign of the reverence with which the village submits to the castle is the readiness of the women to satisfy the desires of the officials. It is an honour for a woman to be summoned by a secretary. The barmaid Frieda is proud to be Klamm's mistress. Gardena, the hostess at the Bridge Inn, lives on her memories of Klamm's love for her twenty years before. Seen through the eyes of the villagers the castle is remote and inaccessible, inscrutable, immanent in the village, all-powerful and beyond moral judgement: it is tantamount to a divinity. It hardly need be said that it recalls the father figures in Kafka's early work. Those who accept its decrees without much question know few intellectual or spiritual problems. Like the peasants of Zürau seen through Kafka's eyes, they are relatively content in their acceptance of a force which to an outsider is a challenge and a threat.

K. receives messages which are apparently from Klamm, brought by a young man, Barnabas. Eager to make contact with Klamm, K. follows Barnabas, who goes, not to the castle, but home to his parents and

The Castle from *Drawings to Kafka* by Yosl Bergnes
'But on approaching it he was disappointed in the castle, it was after all only a wretched looking town.'

sisters. The story of this family is told to K. one night by Barnabas's sister Olga; this tale, which forms an independent whole, has a bearing on K.'s situation. Once respected, the family is now ostracized by the village. For one daughter, Amalia, refused a summons from an official who felt a sudden desire for her. Amalia, a dignified but solitary figure, remains obstinate in her defiance of the castle and of public opinion. She and her family become social outcasts, not because the castle does anything, but because of their own inability to live with a sense of guilt and shame. Had they been able to come to terms with Amalia's action, says Olga, had they not suffered from bad consciences, the villagers would have respected them. But the father's whole concern is to beg forgiveness from the castle for a crime about which it apparently cares nothing. Olga takes to consorting with castle servants in the hope of gaining access to higher officials who might have some jurisdiction in this matter of guilt. Barnabas volunteers as a castle messenger for the same reason, and is neither accepted nor rejected, but left frustrated and ignorant. The first task he is given is to deliver a letter to K. Ironically both K. and Barnabas see in each other a promise of contact with the castle: to K. Barnabas is an official messenger who belongs to the castle and speaks with Klamm; Barnabas thinks that by taking messages to K. he may become an official messenger and pass beyond the outer limits of the castle. For he has never progressed beyond the outermost office, and is not sure whether he has ever met Klamm.

There is a parallel between Barnabas and K., and a similarity and contrast between Amalia and K. Amalia refused to obey a castle official and outraged public opinion. To all appearances she does not recognize any guilt; Olga says she is not subject to fear or impatience. K., too, seems to the villagers to be a rebel, but it is his persistence and childish impatience that distresses them. It is difficult to decide whether the castle is fundamentally benevolent or hostile, or simply indifferent towards K. Amalia's action may be seen as rebellion against an authority that transcends moral judgement, or as an act of heroism in defiance of a perverted power. Our judgement of K. and of the castle is open to as many variations as that of Joseph K. and the court in *The Trial*. To ask whether the castle is good or evil does not lead us very far. K. seeks in an aggressive and wily manner to be accepted into the society of the village and of the castle, and on his own terms, even though he is not completely sure what these terms are, as he is ignorant of the workings of the castle. His is a quest for integration: he wishes to have his own

The two assistants, from a BBC television film of *The Castle*, presented for the centenary of Kafka's birth in 1974

identity and function confirmed by the authorities and by the villagers. Nothing forces him to stay in the village, but he refuses to leave it. He is deprived of certainty, partly at least, because the castle mirrors uncertainty and echoes his lies. The only time he makes direct contact with the interior of the castle, by telephone, he conceals his identity, so that the reply he receives need not apply to him at all. He says he is one of his old assistants and is told that his master can never enter the castle. Despite the ironic humour of such a situation, it is perhaps not only K. who is consumed by an earnest and feverish passion for union. Officials fear meetings with the public lest the strict and difficult rules of bureaucratic etiquette be broken, yet Bürgel reveals that they also secretly long to meet petitioners on human terms, to transcend the rules and be of genuine help. He speaks of this dream of true contact in erotic terms, reflecting on the suicidal happiness of such an event. Bürgel has been caught unawares by K., who enters by mistake the room where he sleeps, but K. is so tired during this curious encounter that he wants only to fall asleep on Bürgel's bed. Thus K.'s weariness deprives both him and Bürgel of the fulfilment of their deepest illicit longings.

One message to K., reputedly from Klamm, could be taken to suggest that K. would do well to concentrate on a limited objective and on setting up house with the barmaid Frieda. But the inconsistency of

Frieda's character, though true to life, is no less a mystery than the castle itself. In any case, K. has a different aim in mind, and sees only derision in the message, or at best a complete misunderstanding. Nor does he recognize that he might learn something about himself from the antics of the two assistants sent to him from the castle. Distorted mirror-images of K., they seem to underline the pointlessness of his striving for more than immediate physical satisfaction.

Much is left undetermined when the novel comes to a premature end, after K. has been in the village for something like a week, a week that is described at greater length than was needed to narrate Karl Rossman's progress across half America or one year in the life of Joseph K. As edited by Brod, the novel is divided into chapters that do not correspond with the divisions in Kafka's manuscript. Brod's report that Kafka planned to end the novel with the death of the hero, after which a message from the castle was to arrive, stating that he could not be recognized as an official surveyor, but allowing him to live and work in the village, does, however, seem plausible. Such an ending would be as non-committal as the existing fragment. There is little sign that K. is any nearer to his goal or that he has changed in any significant way, although after the loss of his mistress Frieda he does come to recognize at least one of his faults. In conversation with Pepi, a caricatured embodiment of his own ambition, K. states that they both suffer from anxiety and impatience which distort their view of matters. Joseph K. had come to a similar conclusion about himself just before his execution. Kafka himself believed that anxiety and impatience characterized his own attitude to reality, but this did not make it any easier for him to come to terms with family, society or life. K. has some faith in Frieda and is charitable towards her when she leaves him: he dismisses Pepi's scorn for her rival; but there are few indications that he has any faith in the castle, or that his attitude of distrust has changed fundamentally. He seems less aggressive in the last chapters, but this may simply be the result of his weariness. His quest for certainty and knowledge appears doomed to failure. To fit into the castle's scheme of things he must know what this scheme is, and what the castle is. In that sense he is indeed one who has come to survey the land and to take its measure. The word used by Kafka's hero to describe himself, *Landvermesser*, has other verbal associations: it might suggest a person who makes a mistake in measurement, or who is presumptuous (*sich vermessen*). The possible ambiguity may well be deliberate. Certainly throughout the novel Kafka provides equally convincing alternative explanations for many details. Each small ambiguity mirrors a yet more fundamental one and contributes to the extraordinary depth and richness of the work.

Is the power with which K. is locked in wilful combat divine or satanic? Is it society, or is it a projection of his own ego? At what level of reality or unreality does it exist? Various answers are possible, and the choice between them depends largely on the expectations or hopes of the answerer. K. has been seen as a Jew seeking a domicile among Gentiles, as an outsider longing for integration, as a man in search of divine grace, and as an intellectual or an artist groping for the truth. Some commentators have believed that K.'s ultimate goal is good, but have disagreed as to whether he fails tragically or achieves some kind of insight. Possibly there is a suggestion that he cannot expect to know more than he knows himself, that, like Joseph K., he may rely too much on the help others might give him. Klamm's letter states that he is appointed surveyor, 'as he knows', and this is as much certainty as is ever given; these words would confirm his belief if it were a firm one, but since he has doubts they only increase his uncertainty. Perhaps as K. became more aware of his impotence he was to learn to live with his ignorance, but he might equally well feel more and more frustration and despair. Those critics who have found Christian meaning in the novel have made much of Kafka's sympathy for the theology of Kierkegaard or of parallels with the existentialist theology of Karl Barth, itself influenced by Kierkegaard. Others, concentrating on the undoubtedly unattractive aspects of the castle, regard K.'s quest as deplorably mistaken, a search for a false religion, a fascination with corruption, and understand the novel as an expression of perverted belief, in the author or in his age. Yet others have seen the work as a parody of mystical thought and a revelation of the folly of irrationalism; but those who have argued thus have not all agreed that this was Kafka's intention, and some hold that he unwittingly exposed the madness of his own belief. All these interpretations look for metaphysical meaning. Some commentators have, however, restricted their vision to the worldly level and taken K. as one searching simply for social integration. Any society may, indeed, be as full of contradictions and shortcomings, and ultimately as mysterious as that which is ruled by the castle, and yet the individual may long to be part of it. Can any person know for certain how he stands in the eyes of others, or who determines what his image is, and can a reputation ever be secure? How do we know what the world thinks us to be, or what our role in society is? K.'s uncertainty can be explained in this way. He may be no more than an exaggerated embodiment of every individual's conflicting desires to be free, and at the same time a part of a greater whole. K. comes to realize, while waiting for Klamm in the Herrenhof courtyard, that freedom born of defiance brings little emotional satisfaction. Whether his yearning for union and acceptance is praiseworthy is a question that cannot be answered in terms of the novel. But it is perhaps suggested that K. longs for love as well as authoritative recognition: when lying in wait for Klamm in his sleigh he tastes Klamm's brandy and is overcome by bliss, a feeling which is compared to the euphoria felt by one who is praised by someone dear to him.

The novel confuses, challenges and fascinates. The dialogue is often lengthy and labyrinthine, full of sudden changes of direction; like a detective story, *The Castle* baffles the reader with conflicting evidence – but there is no final enlightening chapter. Indeed it seems the further the story progresses, the less we know for certain, and we are not even sure what we should be looking for. Kafka deprives us of our usual frame of reference and leaves us as disorientated as his hero. Yet he concentrates on K.'s struggle rather than its hopelessness, and compels us to look forward to the next puzzling episode and to press on hopefully with the hero. He translates K.'s isolation into vivid images. The situations are at once desperately serious and absurdly comic. Once the reader can take the attitude that everything in the book is absurd, K. and the castle, characters, plot, conversations, all ridiculous, then it is nothing but one farcical scene after another narrated with deadpan earnestness. Almost all the elements of Kafka's narrative and all his themes are combined in this one novel. In *The Trial* psychological, social and religious strands appear to be intertwined; here they are fused into one. The individual's search for his role in the world, in his own mind, in the eyes of others and of the ultimate authority, have become aspects of one situation. Mental, emotional, spiritual and physical experiences are not distinguished one from the other in this powerful expression of Kafka's vision of the world. Ultimately *The Castle* makes sense, not because it explains or solves anything, but because it presents a problem: the problem of a man who looks for confirmation of something that can never be known for sure.

It is widely agreed that *The Castle* is Kafka's greatest work. To base a whole conception of Kafka's meaning or message on one possible interpretation of this novel is, however, a dubious procedure, but one which some critics have adopted. It is not Kafka's final summing-up, it is an exploratory work, and not his last. Nor is it in every way representative of his whole œuvre. Some critics, fascinated by the uniqueness of his writings, have maintained that there is no progression in his work. But this is not entirely true, for he varies his approach to related problems, and *The Metamorphosis* and *America* are different from *The Castle*. Kafka's last novel is essentially an elaboration of *Before the Law*, but there is a difference in perspective between it and *The Trial*: there is a distinction between a man who stands accused and one who seeks recognition. Kafka's reputation should not stand or fall by one incomplete novel. Many of his shorter pieces have a completeness lacking in the novels, and for all their brevity and apparent simplicity some of his unpolished sketches are astonishingly rich in content. As one of Kafka's detractors, Edmund Wilson, noted, the best of his short stories are first-rate works of literature, whereas a fragmentary novel, however impressive, cannot be compared with a complete one. Nevertheless there is a sense in which all Kafka's work is fragmentary, and *The Castle* perhaps best reveals the stature of this fragment. For if, as we suspect, Kafka aimed to give a complete impression and explanation of the world as he saw it, he was, because of the magnitude of the task, and because of his own uncertainty, doomed to failure. But few will measure Kafka's work by the standards he set himself.

The winter of 1922–3 and the following spring Kafka spent in Prague. His health was poor; he spent much of his time in bed. His pension was small and he was worried about the cost of medical attention. His mother underwent an operation in December and he was concerned about her slow recovery. In November he complained of monotony relieved only by visits from Brod, in March of having gone through periods of madness, and in June 1923 he wrote in his diary: 'The horrible spells recently, innumerable, almost without pause. Walks, nights, days, incapable of anything but pain.' He was corresponding intermittently with Brod, Robert Klopstock, Oskar Baum and Minze E. He must have begun several stories, but destroyed all but three pieces: *Das Ehepaar* (*The Married Couple*), *Gib's auf!* (*Give it up!*) and *Von den Gleichnissen* (*On Parables*).

In the first of these a businessman visits a customer in his home at an unusual and inopportune moment. He begins, with an energetic lack of tact, to persuade the ageing customer, who is tired and occupied with his private affairs, to agree to a deal. This is too much for the old man, who promptly dies of a heart attack. His wife, however, maintains that he is asleep, and brings him back to life. The old man gets into bed with his son who is lying sick in the room. The businessman leaves defeated and despondent, with a feeling of loss and isolation. For he has seen a miracle wrought by the wife on her husband, by a woman who reminds him of his own mother who died when he was a child. The businessman is excluded from family love that unites husband and wife, and, equally significantly in the context of Kafka's life, father and son. Kafka's return to his parental home had evidently reminded him forcibly of his old preoccupations with the ideal of domestic happiness. *Give it up!* is a short sketch devoid of all ornament and comment. A man on his way to the station in a strange town notices that he has less time than he thought, becomes anxious and unsure of himself, and asks a policeman the way:

> He smiled and said, 'You asking me the way?' 'Yes,' I said, 'since I can't find it myself.' 'Give it up! Give it up!' said he, and turned with a sudden jerk like someone who wants to be alone with his laughter.

The representative of the law will not or cannot help the anxious individual. *On Parables* is an intellectual joke with a serious basis, such as might be popular among students of rabbinical law. It begins with a comment on the figurative language of wise men which refers to a sphere of existence or a level of meaning beyond the understanding of ordinary men:

> All these parables really set out to say merely that the incomprehensible is incomprehensible, and that we know already. But the cares we have to struggle with every day: that is a different matter.
> Concerning this a man once said: Why such reluctance? If you only followed the parables you yourselves would become parables and with that rid of all your daily cares.
> Another said: I bet this is also a parable.
> The first said: You have won.
> The second said: But unfortunately only in parable.
> The first said: No, in reality: in parable you have lost.

The limitations of action, thought and language combine to create confusion, frustration, and a smile of resignation.

In July 1923 Kafka was well enough to take a holiday in Müritz, a resort on the Baltic, with his sister Elli. To Klopstock he wrote that he had escaped the ghosts that pursued him. 'Through the trees I can see the children playing. Happy, healthy, passionate children – when I am among them I am not happy but stand on the threshold of happi-

Dora Diamant

ness' (BR. 436). These children can hardly have been less noisy than others who had tortured him before, yet they had a special value for him as a reminder of joy and life; besides they came from a holiday centre belonging to that Jewish People's Home in Berlin in which Felice Bauer had once worked. Kafka spent much of his time in this colony, took part in its religious life and became quite attached to at least one of the children. Here was a real community which he was privileged to visit as a guest. The symbol of the ideal community that he called Palestine was beyond his reach, but this self-contained Jewish colony, dedicated to its own integrity, could offer him glimpses of the Promised Land. Among the helpers there was a girl of about twenty-two who was fascinated by Kafka and impressed by his love of children before she knew who he was. She came from a family of Hassidic Polish Jews and was open and generous by nature. She shared with Kafka an interest in the Hebrew language, with which he had been struggling for years and which he was now studying with some zeal. Her Hassidic background, which he had always associated with a truly religious acceptance of life, attracted him. He left Müritz determined to live with this girl, Dora Diamant (or Dymant) in Berlin.

A page of Hebrew exercises done by Kafka

His parents could scarcely have approved of this plan and he stayed only a few days in Prague. His sister Ottla, however, with whom he now spent a few weeks in Schelesen, probably encouraged him in his intention, and in late September he was in Berlin with Dora. Berlin had always attracted him. In his early dreams of escape from Prague he had preferred Berlin to Vienna as a possible goal. He seems to have associated Vienna with decadence, and Berlin with crass vitality, the reality of modern life. Now it promised to bring him, as he wrote to Robert Klopstock, quite close to the Jews (BR. 442). In Berlin, indeed, he attended classes on the Talmud and read some easier Hebrew texts.

E. L. Kirchner *Street Scene* c.1914

These activities can scarcely have satisfied his longing for community, but his yearning for the simple pleasures of a home of his own were answered through Dora Diamant, and Brod observed that this was, thanks to her, the happiest period of Kafka's life. To his sister Valli he wrote a moving objective description of his domestic scene. There was no luxury, for the couple had little money and it was a time of severe inflation. It was perhaps the very absence of bourgeois trappings that so pleased him. Bourgeois respectability was also lacking. The couple had to leave their first flat because the landlady disapproved of their household. For a few weeks after the move to Berlin, which he described as a mad venture comparable to Napoleon's invasion of Russia (br. 447), he slept well; but by mid-October his 'ghosts' had caught up with him. The domestic idyll was overshadowed by his illness and by the economic situation. Max Brod believed that the physical hardships that Kafka suffered during this winter had a fatal effect on his health. The couple could afford nothing except food, and that was often hard to get. He gave up buying newspapers as an economy measure, but was reluctant to receive gifts of food and money from Prague. Rather, he instructed his sister Elli to send gift parcels to poor Jewish children, and Dora presented home-made cakes to a Jewish orphanage. The couple were forced to move flat again in February 1924 because they could not pay the rent which, like other prices, increased astronomically with every month. Brod noted that his friend was deeply hurt by the sufferings of the poor around him. Kafka himself believed, as always, that his physical deterioration had inner causes, and complained that he could not afford to be ill, rather than that poverty aggravated his condition. But ill he was, and ever more seriously. At first he spent his mornings in bed and went for short walks in the afternoon. Scarcely once did he go into the city except to attend lectures at the Jewish High School. By March he had not been outside the house for weeks.

Under his instructions Dora Diamant destroyed some of his manuscripts and only two stories written in Berlin have survived. *Eine kleine Frau* (*A Little Woman*) may reflect Kafka's experience of his landlady; it is an extended consideration of the problem posed by a woman's strong disapproval of the narrator. He is oversensitive to her attitude and overscrupulous in his analysis of it. He decides that he must bear with the problem and attempt to minimize its importance. Strangely enough this rather dry monologue was prepared by Kafka for publication in the *Hunger Artist* collection, whereas the more impressive

Der Bau (*The Burrow*) was passed over. *The Burrow* is a long series of reflections linked to a minimum of action, rather like *Investigations of a Dog*, but without so much humour. The themes of curiosity and frustration are subordinated to a sense of dread. An animal (perhaps a mole or a badger) has devoted the best part of his life to constructing an intricate burrow designed to protect him from attack. He gains some satisfaction from his work and enjoys solitude and peace in his underground existence. Yet he knows that the burrow is an inadequate protection. He senses that the dangers of the outside world, from which he has escaped, may be more numerous, but cannot be as terrible as the threat of attack in his burrow. His fear has been simplified but intensified. The story breaks off as the animal is mentally paralysed by fear of a suspicious and inexplicable noise that permeates his burrow. Dora Diamant declared that a lost final passage showed the animal's death in combat with the attacker. Kafka's preoccupation with his own situation and with his literary activity is reflected in the interconnection of solitude and fear, fear for the self and fear for the life's work which has been created as a form of self-defence but exposes its creator to fatal danger. Yet as always in Kafka's stories more general interpretations are possible. The fragment suggests that it is fatal to shut oneself off from the world and to indulge in self-examination, even if it brings a sense of satisfaction. Objective evaluation of one's own work is in any case impossible. The animal goes outside his burrow to survey it through the eyes of others, but realizes that without his presence in it it is not the same burrow. The threat from within the earth around the burrow appears to be everywhere at once; it is perhaps a transcendental danger. *The Burrow*, like most of Kafka's late works, is characterized by tireless intellectual probing.

Kafka did not divulge to his friend or to his family the seriousness of his condition. But they became aware of it. In March 1924 Kafka's uncle Siegfried, the doctor, went to Berlin and decided that Kafka had to be taken to a sanatorium. He and Brod took him back to Prague. Dora Diamant followed a few days later. Kafka returned to his parents' home; his last attempt at independence had ended in ignominious defeat, yet he knew that he was dying and occasionally allowed himself the luxury of tyrannical behaviour. His throat burnt when he drank, and he suspected that his larynx was infected. His voice was weak, and to Robert Klopstock, who had abandoned his studies in Berlin to be with him, he remarked that he had just written a story about animal squeakings. The word that he used, *piepsen*, describes the chirping or squeaking of small birds or animals, but also means to feel poorly. Kafka was referring to his last story, *Josephine oder das Volk der Mäuse* (*Josephine, or the Mice Nation*).

This tale, which was included in the *Hunger Artist* collection, is permeated by irony; its questions and counter questions, assertions and retractions almost cancel each other out. The plot is minimal and the subject-matter apparently absurd. Yet the very absurdity and the flashes of humour, often based on word-plays, lead the reader on to become intrigued by the paradoxes. He senses the involvement of the author who strives to give an impression of ironic detachment, and a deadly seriousness behind the playful manipulation. Josephine, the singing mouse, seems the very opposite of the hunger artist. Her piping is no different from the sounds emitted all the time by other mice, yet it unites the mice in a sense of community. Apparently it is her (probably deluded) belief in her own art that fascinates and awes others. The community allows her certain privileges, but stops short of recognizing her as someone quite different from all others. This is what she desires, and in trying to force this recognition from the community she makes her great mistake. She attempts to dictate to society by refusing to sing, but the nation of mice can exist without her and probably does not need her art to express its community spirit. She is defeated, yet at the same time liberated, free to claim her exemption from common laws, even if only in death. The individual who presumes to be different is free to be so in death. There was a hint of such liberation in the ending of *The Judgement*, and one of Kafka's diary entries of 1917 suggests that he could then welcome the prospect of death as a bringer of reconciliation. In death the individual might be submerged in the whole, the community or creation, the whole which Kafka felt he had left but to which he longed to return, and which he linked with the name of the father: 'I would then put myself into the hands of death. Remnant of a faith. Return to the father. *Grosser Versöhnungstag* (Great Day of Atonement or Reconciliation)' (T. Sept/Oct '17). Josephine's revolt against the community may be seen as that of the artist or would-be misfit, the arrogant outsider rebelling against laws which are social, existential or metaphysical. According to our interpretation of the law or custom that she finds intolerable – it is the law that every mouse must do everyday work – our evaluation of her demand will differ. Kafka's ironic prevarication allows for such differences. Yet it is perhaps significant that in this last work he views his fictional animal and artist from the standpoint of a member of the community,

A photograph taken for Kafka's last passport

and nevertheless passes a not totally negative judgement on one who claims to be an exception.

When Kafka was admitted to a sanatorium near Vienna, the doctors confirmed that his larynx had been infected by T.B. He was promptly transferred, as a difficult if not impossible case, to the university clinic in Vienna. Now he could scarcely eat or talk above a whisper and was drugged. Nevertheless he was conscious of the world around him, and witnessed the death of a fellow patient in the bed beside his in the open ward. He was moved again to a more comfortable, private sanatorium in Kierling near Klosterneuburg. There he had a room to himself, full of flowers and with a view on to the countryside. Specialist after specialist confirmed that nothing could be done for him except relieve his pain. But each new drug had only a temporary effect. In May Brod visited his friend to learn that Dora's father had refused to agree to her marriage to Kafka. Whether Kafka desired marriage for her sake is not known, but he accepted her father's decision as binding. He had written to her father, admitting that he was not a practising Jew, but claiming that he was seeking conversion and might therefore be acceptable to a pious family. The father consulted his rabbi, who was believed by the Hassidic community to have miraculous powers. The rabbi said no, and, as was his custom, gave no explanation. Kafka was impressed by this answer and took it as a bad omen.

He dissuaded his parents from making the journey from Prague, saying that he was no worse than before. But to the two young people beside him, whom he called his family, he cried out in pain. Dora and Robert Klopstock took turns to sit with him. Those who saw him in these last weeks of his life testify to his courage, and those who had not known him before were impressed by his personality. His thoughts seem to have been directed towards life. He recalled his youthful impressions of his father, and of one of his cousins who had also represented to him the vitality that he believed he lacked himself. Towards the end he could communicate only by means of written notes, several of which reveal an intense concern for the well-being of the flowers in his room. He was struck by the contrast between the flowers' thirst for water and his own inability to take more than a painful sip. They appeared oblivious of their own death: 'How marvellous that is, don't you think? The lilac – it drinks as it dies, it is still swilling it down. That is impossible, that a dying man should drink' (BR. 491). He appears to have been anxious to live life as fully as possible until the last minute. Yet his enjoyment of a few pieces of fruit, a yoghourt, a sip of water, or even of beer, was invariably marred by pain in his throat. So, too, the comfort given by the presence of Dora and Robert Klopstock was accompanied by the knowledge that they were suffering with him. The following note must have been addressed to one of them: 'How many years will you stand it? How long shall I bear you standing it?' (BR. 487) Even to the last he remained the professional slave to language, discerning its inability to cope with the paradoxes of reality. In the week before he died he was correcting the proofs of *A Hunger Artist*, and in his last hours he cried out to Robert Klopstock, 'Kill me, or you are a murderer'. For even morphia could not relieve his pain.

Kafka died on 3 June 1924, one month before his forty-first birthday. On 11 June he was buried in the Jewish cemetery in Prague. His parents were buried there a few years later. Dora Diamant, Max Brod, and several others who had known Kafka, left Germany in the 1930s. Dora Diamant died in England in 1952, Max Brod made a distinguished career in Israel. Kafka's three sisters died in concentration camps.

George Grosz *Funeral Procession* 1917

A host of perspectives

Kafka's anxiety and insecurity provide abundant material for psycho-
analytical comment and theory. The pathological features of his
personality are clear enough; they are, however, all too easily distorted
and trivialized by inadequate terminology. For words such as father-
complex, in so far as they promise explanation and clarification and
offer simplification, can be misleading. There are almost as many
paradoxes in Kafka the man as in his writing. An introvert, he was full
of consideration for others and deeply interested in the world around
him. His isolation was forced upon him, yet he clung to it. He saw
complications where they did not exist, and retreated in fear from
largely imagined conflicts and from situations that an ordinary person
would have taken in his stride. Yet he lived bravely with his weaknesses.
In company he could veil his profound uncertainty in an air of calm.
He bore his anxieties and faced his illness and the prospect of premature death with great fortitude. His despair was tempered by humour
and renunciation. Believing himself incapable of coping with the rigours
of ordinary life, he yet dedicated himself to the formidable task of
discovering and revealing the truths of existence. An overactive mind
almost destroyed him, yet this same mind probed further than that of
more normal and happier individuals. His great sensitivity, keen intellect

and fertile imagination were psychologically destructive but artistically . creative. Intense emotion and apathy, exhilaration and depression, hope and despair coloured his life. Little wonder that his character calls forth wonder, admiration, abhorrence and rejection.

Many readers have undoubtedly dismissed Kafka's novels and stories as pernicious outpourings of a deranged soul. Among writers and critics, however, such a reaction has been relatively rare, and most have recognized him, for different reasons, as one of the greatest writers of this century, gifted with extraordinary insight and powers of expression. His long, often tortuous, sentences and dialogues have so impressed many critics that they have assumed that Kafka's style is essentially one of long, intricate periods. Amplification and qualification are, indeed, an important characteristic of his work and vividly express uncertainty and confusion. Yet his long sentences are invariably balanced by short ones, labyrinthine conversations and involved reflections by lively description, tense action and striking incident. The multiplicity of interpretations of his work that have been offered arises directly from the character of his writing.

On his death Kafka's few published works were known mainly among Jewish intellectuals in Prague and Vienna. He was seen as a writer of promise. Curiously, in view of later reactions, his subject-matter occasioned little surprise, and it was his style that impressed readers. Even when Brod published the three unfinished novels in the mid twenties, they made little impact on the German-speaking world. The first edition of Kafka's collected works which appeared under Brod's supervision in the thirties was banned by the Nazis. Not until after the Second World War, therefore, when he was already the object of a cult in certain circles in France, Britain and America, did Kafka become widely known in Germany. Brod's enthusiasm went largely unheeded. In his postscript to *The Castle* he claimed that this novel could be compared with Goethe's *Faust*, that the castle represented grace, as the court in *The Trial* stood for the other aspect of the Jewish God, justice. Kafka's central theme was the gulf between the human and divine worlds. This reading of Kafka was to be followed and elaborated by many commentators. The first of these, and the most influential, was Edwin Muir, who introduced Kafka to the English public. Greatly impressed by Kafka's work and struck by its resemblance to his own writing, Muir undertook its translation as a labour of love. *The Castle*, translated by Edwin and Willa Muir, appeared in 1930. Muir asserted that this novel and *The Trial* are metaphysical or theological works. He called Kafka's technique allegorical and thus determined many subsequent attempts to interpret Kafka. Like Brod, he placed Kafka in the context of a general European crisis of belief. Numerous critics were later to talk of Kafka's religious belief or despair, and to link his work with Pascal or Kierkegaard, Karl Barth's crisis theology, with the Cabbala and with Christian mystics. The majority thought that he was tortured by the absence of God in the post-Nietzschean age, although Brod and Muir had taken him to suggest the possibility of belief in an era of doubt.

The English writers of the thirties were at first repulsed by what they saw as Kafka's destructive individualism, but after the Spanish Civil War, their Marxist idealism somewhat tarnished, they celebrated him as a great explorer of solitude and despair. The sociological approach to Kafka, already suggested by Brod, had begun. He was seen as alienated from society and a social critic. After his reputation had been made in the West, critics in eastern Europe developed this line in more detail. Communists who had taken Kafka as the typical product of a diseased society now saw him as a critic of capitalism. The psychological aspects of Kafka's alienation became clearer after 1937, when Brod published the diaries and his biography of his friend. Again it was after the war that psychological interpretations of Kafka proliferated. In extreme cases, his narratives were explained as systematic exemplifications of Freudian or Jungian theories and ransacked for sexual symbols. The element of the subconscious, the dreamlike quality of Kafka's writings had impressed the Surrealists in France in the late thirties. The Surrealists went further than Kafka in following irrational association in their art, but the insect of *The Metamorphosis* is as ghastly, and Odradek (a being something like two sticks attached to a cotton-reel in *The Cares of the Family Man*) as curious as any painting by Salvador Dali.

Before 1939 Kafka was discovered by writers and intellectuals in England and France, and already his impact on other novelists began to be felt, but he had scarcely reached a more general public. During and immediately after the war his visions of helplessness and horror and of authoritarian bureaucracy gained a baleful meaning, and it was widely felt that he had in some mysterious way foreseen the horrors of the Nazi period and of the war. Since Kafka so often portrays man as the victim of demonic forces it was almost inevitable that a link would be forged between his writings and the holocausts experienced by his readers. Frenchmen particularly saw mirrored in his work their impotence and frustration under the Nazi occupation. The Existentialists referred to Kafka as a forerunner of their own manner of thinking and writing. Sartre reportedly admitted that he had been influenced by Kafka, and there are indeed similarities between Kafka's heroes and the outsiders of the novels of Sartre and Camus. Recognition of the absurdity of life and the weariness and disgust attendant upon this recognition linked Kafka with Existentialism. Camus wrote of Kafka as one of the few writers who had seen human life in its basic absurdity, an absurdity which, according to Camus, arises from our desire to make sense of a world that refuses to yield a meaning. Critics soon found detailed resemblances between Kafka and Kierkegaard, Dostoyevsky, Husserl and Jaspers, and Kafka was included in anthologies of Existentialist writings. But, to judge from his writings, he never committed himself to any of the many ways of living with absurdity suggested by other Existentialists.

Camus also maintained that Kafka's symbolism could not be exhausted by any one interpretation. As more and more commentators put forward various apparently contradictory readings of Kafka, many of them plausible but almost all dubious in detail, the ambiguity of his work became more and more apparent. It was recognized by Edwin Muir who became dissatisfied with his earlier statement about Kafka's allegorical technique. Yet articles and books claiming that Kafka meant this or that continued to proliferate. The adjective Kafkaesque was much used and abused. The mystery that had been explained in so many ways was still a mystery. Kafka, whose *Castle* had been taken by Muir as a modern *Pilgrim's Progress*, and who inspired Rex Warner to write an allegorical novel, struck the French novelist Robbe-Grillet as an author who had mastered the technique of presenting phenomena without suggesting a 'higher reality' or meaning behind them. Other critics have suggested that Kafka was writing about the difficulty of writing. This interpretation is plausible, for this theme has preoccupied other authors of Kafka's time and since, particularly in Germany; it involves questions about the reality to be represented, as well as methods of representation. Yet no one systematic interpretation has been able to pin down all the possible meanings of Kafka's work. His lucidity was that of a man who saw many sides to questions that he could not resolve. He has been extolled as a thinker, yet his thoughts, as recorded in aphorisms, letters or diaries, are full of paradox, contradiction and ambivalence. Part of his uniqueness as a writer is that his work contains so many facets and so little certainty. Stylistic analyses of his writing have revealed more and more aspects of his irony and ambiguity.

'The right perception of a matter and a misunderstanding of the same matter do not wholly exclude each other', says the chaplain to Joseph K. in *The Trial*. Perhaps the interpretations of Kafka, apparently as mutually contradictory as the commentaries on the story of the doorkeeper that occasion the chaplain's remark, contain part of the truth, are not completely false, but are misunderstandings in so far as they are one-sided. Perhaps many of them are valid, in essence if not in detail. Another dictum of Kafka's might encourage us to believe that taken together the various commentaries give a fuller and truer picture than any one of them alone. He wrote that one person cannot express the truth, but that a host of perspectives might come closer to this goal (H. 343). Was not Kafka searching for something that would give meaning to all the aspects of life as he saw it, to interrelate religious, psychological, social and artistic problems? 'This fear is perhaps not only fear, but at the same time a longing for something', he wrote to Milena (BrM. 249). He longed for a system of thought or belief that would transcend the distinctions between the various compartments of life. It was such a faith that gave meaning to every detail of existence which he envied in the Hassidic Jews. It may be that he sensed, but would not accept, the limitations of reason, and knew in his heart that only faith, which he thought was denied him, could answer his longing. The most memorable of his heroes attempt in vain to discover the truth about themselves or the world through reason, and are particularly incensed by apparent illogicalities.

Since the fifties we have become more used to the literature of query and symbol and more prepared to understand Kafka as one of its founders. We are able to see him in the contexts of the collapse of religious and humanitarian faith and of Prague as a hotbed of alienation. But to equate him with any one philosophical school or artistic movement, Existentialism, Expressionism, Surrealism, is to underestimate him. Only by taking all such analogies, and the many meanings of his work, together can we approach a just evaluation of his historical significance.

If Kafka shares thoughts and feelings with many twentieth-century writers and philosophers, it is because he experienced similar doubts. He felt, with excruciating personal involvement, and expressed, earlier than most and with a compelling vividness equalled by none, the loss of a convincing belief that could give meaning to life. Religion and science, faith and reason seemed unobtainable or inadequate. Everything was relative and there was no universal system of order. The various ways of seeing reality were no longer personal variations within a given universal system; specialists had created their own separate disciplines that seemed to bear no relation to each other. There were many possible meanings, but no one meaning. In *Those Barren Leaves*, Aldous Huxley has Calamy reflect on this situation as he contemplates his hand: in it an infant sees only a shape, a physicist atoms and fields of energy, a chemist electrons and molecules; its owner thinks of it as an implement for good or evil and an erotic tool – but where is the common denominator? Calamy is fascinated by this question, and not driven to distraction by it, yet his intellectual reaction is not so different from that occasioned by Kafka's writing:

> 'It is extraordinary,' Calamy went on, 'what a lot of different modes of existence a thing has, when you come to think about it. And the more you think, the more obscure and mysterious everything becomes. What seemed solid vanishes; what was obvious and comprehensible becomes utterly mysterious. Gulfs begin opening all around you – more and more abysses, as though the ground were splitting in an earthquake. It gives one a strange sense of insecurity, of being in the dark.'*

Questions like Calamy's were put again and again by Kafka, less clearly, less philosophically, veiled in narrative and symbol, but burning with a greater emotional urgency. They are likely to concern men at any time, but are particularly distressing in an age when faith has collapsed and total answers are suspect. Kafka's importance consists in having raised questions of this order, not as an intellectual exercise, but in a manner that expresses the emotional and spiritual basis of man's longing for certainty and synthesis. He gives, not an interpretation of the world, but a reflection of a world in which there is desperate need for a synthesis of many interpretations, each of which is doubted. He exposes the apparent absurdity of reality, and equally the absurdity of the human mind that judges it to be absurd.

* Aldous Huxley, *Those Barren Leaves*, London (Chatto & Windus), 1925, p. 343. Reprinted by courtesy of Mrs Laura Huxley and Chatto & Windus.

Bibliography

KAFKA'S WORKS

Betrachtung Leipzig 1913
Der Heizer, Ein Fragment Leipzig 1913
Die Verwandlung Leipzig 1915
Das Urteil, Eine Geschichte Leipzig 1916
In der Strafkolonie Leipzig 1919
Ein Landarzt, Kleine Erzählungen Leipzig/Munich 1919
Ein Hungerkünstler, Vier Geschichten Berlin 1924

POSTHUMOUS PUBLICATIONS ed Max Brod
Der Prozess Berlin 1925
Das Schloss Munich 1926
Amerika Munich 1927
Beim Bau der chinesischen Mauer, Ungedrückte Erzählungen und Prosa aus dem Nachlass Berlin 1931

COLLECTED WORKS ed. Max Brod
Gesammelte Schriften (first edition)
  I *Erzählungen und kleine Prosa* Berlin 1935
  II *Amerika* Berlin 1935

III *Der Prozess* Berlin 1935
IV *Das Schloss* Berlin 1935
V *Beschreibung eines Kampfes. Novellen, Skizzen, Aphorismen aus dem Nachlass* Prague 1936
VI *Tagebücher und Briefe* Prague 1937

Gesammelte Werke (second edition) New York/Frankfurt am Main

Der Prozess 1950
Das Schloss 1951
Tagebücher 1910–1923 1951
Briefe an Milena (ed. W. Haas) 1952
Erzählungen 1952
Amerika 1953
Hochzeitsvorbereitungen auf dem Lande und andere Prosa aus dem Nachlass 1953
Beschreibung eines Kampfes, Novellen, Skizzen, Aphorismen aus dem Nachlass 1954
Briefe 1902–1924 1958
Briefe an Felice (ed. E. Heller, J. Born) 1967

ENGLISH TRANSLATIONS
(by Edwin and Willa Muir, unless otherwise stated)
The Castle London (Secker & Warburg), New York (Knopf) 1930
The Great Wall of China and Other Pieces London (Secker & Warburg), 1933; as *The Great Wall of China. Stories and Reflections* New York (Schocken Books) 1946
The Trial London (Gollancz), New York (Knopf) 1937; London (Secker & Warburg) New York (Knopf) 1945
Parables. In German and English translated by W. and E. Muir, C. Greenberg, New York (Schocken Books) 1947
In the Penal Settlement. Tales and Short Prose Works London (Secker & Warburg) 1949; as *The Penal Colony. Stories and Short Pieces* New York (Schocken Books) 1948
America London (Routledge & Kegan Paul) 1938; New York (Doubleday) 1955
The Diaries volume I, 1910–1913, translated by J. Kresh, London (Secker & Warburg), New York (Schocken Books) 1948; volume II, 1914–1923, translated by M. Greenberg, London (Secker & Warburg), New York (Schocken Books) 1949
Selected Short Stories New York (The Modern Library) 1952
Letters to Milena, translated by T. and J. Stern, London (Secker & Warburg), New York (Schocken Books) 1953

Wedding Preparations in the Country and Other Posthumous Prose Writings, translated by W. and E. Muir, T. and J. Stern, London (Secker & Warburg) 1954

Dearest Father. Stories and Other Writings, translated by E. Kaiser, E. Wilkins, New York (Schocken Books) 1954

Description of a Struggle, translated by T. and J. Stern, New York (Schocken Books) 1958

Description of a Struggle and The Great Wall of China, translated by W. and E. Muir, T. and J. Stern, London (Secker & Warburg) 1960

Letters to Felice, translated by J. Stern, E. Duckworth, New York (Schocken Books) 1973

The Diaries, The Castle, Metamorphosis and Other Stories and *The Trial* have been published in the UK as Penguins.

BIOGRAPHY

Bauer, J. *Kafka und Prag* Stuttgart 1971

Brod, M. *Franz Kafka. Eine Biographie* (third augmented edition) Frankfurt am Main 1954; translated by G. H. Roberts, R. Winston, *A Biography of Franz Kafka* New York 1957

Buber-Neumann, M. *Kafkas, Freundin Milena* Munich 1963

Canetti, E. *Der andere Prozess. Kafkas Briefe an Felice* Munich 1969

Eisner, P. *Franz Kafka and Prague* New York 1950

Frynta, E. *Franz Kafka lebte in Prag* Prague 1960

Janouch, G. *Gespräche mit Kafka* Frankfurt am Main 1951; translated by G. Rees, *Conversations with Kafka* London/New York 1953

Politzer, H. (ed.), *Das Kafka Buch. Eine innere Biographie in Selbstzeugnissen* Frankfurt am Main 1965

Wagenbach, K. *Franz Kafka. Eine Biographie seiner Jugend 1883–1912* Berne 1958; *Franz Kafka in Selbstzeugnissen und Bilddokumenten* Hamburg 1964

ON THE CHRONOLOGY OF KAFKA'S WORKS

M. Pasley, K. Wagenbach, 'Datierung sämtlicher Texte F. Kafkas' in J. Born, L. Dietz, M. Pasley, P. Raabe, K. Wagenbach, *Kafka Symposion* (second edition), Berlin 1966

GENERAL STUDIES OF KAFKA

IN ENGLISH

Anders, G. *Franz Kafka* London/New York 1960

Flores, A. (ed.) *The Kafka Problem* New York 1946

Flores, A., H. Swander (eds.), *Franz Kafka Today* Madison 1958

Foulkes, A. P. *The Reluctant Pessimist. A Study of Franz Kafka* The Hague/ Paris 1967

Gray, R. D. (ed.) *Kafka. A Collection of Critical Essays* Englewood Cliffs 1962

Gray, R. D. *Kafka* Cambridge 1973

Greenberg, M. *The Terror of Art. Kafka and Modern Literature* London 1971

Heller, E. 'The World of Franz Kafka' in his *The Disinherited Mind* London 1952

Neider, C. *The Frozen Sea. A Study of Franz Kafka* New York 1948

Osborne, C. *Kafka* Edinburgh/London 1967

Politzer, H. *Franz Kafka. Parable and Paradox* New York 1966

Sokel, W. H. *Franz Kafka* New York/London 1966

Tauber, H. *Franz Kafka. An Introduction to His Works*, London/Yale 1948

Thorlby, A. *A Students' Guide to Kafka* London 1972

IN GERMAN

Beissner, F. *Der Erzähler Franz Kafka* Stuttgart 1952

Emrich, W. *Franz Kafka* Bonn 1958

Hermsdorf, H. *Kafka* Berlin 1961

Pongs, H. *Franz Kafka, Dichter des Labyrinths* Heidelberg 1960

Reiss, H. S. *Franz Kafka. Eine Betrachtung seines Werkes*, Heidelberg 1952

Richter, H. *Franz Kafka* Berlin 1962

Sokel, W. H. *Franz Kafka. Tragik und Ironie* Munich 1964

Walser, M. *Beschreibung einer Form. Franz Kafka* Munich 1961

Weltsch, F. *Religion und Humor im Leben und Werk Franz Kafkas*, Berlin 1957

IN FRENCH

Albérès, R. M., P. de Boisdeffre *Franz Kafka* Paris 1960

Carrouges, M. *Kafka* Paris 1948

Dentan, M. *Humour et création littéraire dans l'œuvre de Franz Kafka* Geneva 1961

Robert, M. *Kafka* Paris 1960

BIBLIOGRAPHIES

Flores, A. 'Franz Kafka: Biography and Criticism' in his *The Kafka Problem* (reprint) New York 1963

Hemmerle, R. (ed.) *Franz Kafka. Eine Bibliographie* Munich 1957

Järv, H. *Die Kafka-Literatur* Malmö-Lund 1961

Index